Number 127
Fall 2010

New Directions for Evaluation

Sandra Mathison
Editor-in-Chief

Critical Social Theory and Evaluation Practice

Melissa Freeman
Editor

CRITICAL SOCIAL THEORY AND EVALUATION PRACTICE
Melissa Freeman (ed.)
New Directions for Evaluation, no. 127
Sandra Mathison, Editor-in-Chief

Microfilm copies of issues and articles are available in 16mm and 35mm, as well as microfiche in 105mm, through University Microfilms Inc., 300 North Zeeb Road, Ann Arbor, MI 48106-1346.

New Directions for Evaluation is indexed in Cambridge Scientific Abstracts (CSA/CIG), Contents Pages in Education (T & F), Higher Education Abstracts (Claremont Graduate University), Social Services Abstracts (CSA/CIG), Sociological Abstracts (CSA/CIG), and Worldwide Political Sciences Abstracts (CSA/CIG).

NEW DIRECTIONS FOR EVALUATION (ISSN 1097-6736, electronic ISSN 1534-875X) is part of The Jossey-Bass Education Series and is published quarterly by Wiley Subscription Services, Inc., A Wiley Company, at Jossey-Bass, 989 Market Street, San Francisco, CA 94103-1741.

SUBSCRIPTIONS cost $89 for U.S./Canada/Mexico; $113 international. For institutions, agencies, and libraries, $271 U.S.; $311 Canada/Mexico; $345 international. Prices subject to change.

EDITORIAL CORRESPONDENCE should be addressed to the Editor-in-Chief, Sandra Mathison, University of British Columbia, 2125 Main Mall, Vancouver, BC V6T 1Z4, Canada.

www.josseybass.com

Editorial Policy and Procedures

New Directions for Evaluation, a quarterly sourcebook, is an official publication of the American Evaluation Association. The journal publishes empirical, methodological, and theoretical works on all aspects of evaluation. A reflective approach to evaluation is an essential strand to be woven through every issue. The editors encourage issues that have one of three foci: (1) craft issues that present approaches, methods, or techniques that can be applied in evaluation practice, such as the use of templates, case studies, or survey research; (2) professional issues that present topics of import for the field of evaluation, such as utilization of evaluation or locus of evaluation capacity; (3) societal issues that draw out the implications of intellectual, social, or cultural developments for the field of evaluation, such as the women's movement, communitarianism, or multiculturalism. A wide range of substantive domains is appropriate for *New Directions for Evaluation;* however, the domains must be of interest to a large audience within the field of evaluation. We encourage a diversity of perspectives and experiences within each issue, as well as creative bridges between evaluation and other sectors of our collective lives.

The editors do not consider or publish unsolicited single manuscripts. Each issue of the journal is devoted to a single topic, with contributions solicited, organized, reviewed, and edited by a guest editor. Issues may take any of several forms, such as a series of related chapters, a debate, or a long article followed by brief critical commentaries. In all cases, the proposals must follow a specific format, which can be obtained from the editor-in-chief. These proposals are sent to members of the editorial board and to relevant substantive experts for peer review. The process may result in acceptance, a recommendation to revise and resubmit, or rejection. However, the editors are committed to working constructively with potential guest editors to help them develop acceptable proposals.

Sandra Mathison, Editor-in-Chief
University of British Columbia
2125 Main Mall
Vancouver, BC V6T 1Z4
CANADA
e-mail: nde@eval.org

CONTENTS

EDITOR'S NOTES

Since the passage of the Elementary and Secondary Act in 1965, evaluation has played an essential role in political decision making (House, 2005). From its onset, the primary purpose of evaluation has been to determine what works so as to target resources in ways that would produce the desired effects. Evaluation, however, conceived of as a science, found itself enmeshed in positivism's reliance on value-free and objectivist approaches, leading evaluators to believe that values lay outside the purview of their responsibilities (House, 2005). Arguing against this conception of science, House and Howe (1999) demonstrate that facts and values are endpoints of the same continuum and that context, and the people implicated, determine where a statement or perspective gets placed on the fact–value continuum. Tensions and issues surrounding the relationship of research and evaluation to policy making and politics are not new.

> The scientist is called upon to contribute information useful to implement a given policy, but the policy itself is given, not open to question. . . So long as the social scientist continues to accept a role in which he [sic] does not question policies, state problems, and formulate alternatives, the more does he [sic] become routinized in the role of bureaucratic technician. (Merton & Lerner, 1951, p. 306)

Merton and Lerner found that researchers' roles have changed from that of autonomous knowledge generators to one of policy advisors, where policy makers contract and, hence, provide financial support to the research and researcher in question. They concluded that the resources provided by bureaucratic power structures threatened the scientists' ability to question and consider alternative conceptualizations for, or effects of, the policy in question. In other words, this relationship jeopardized the ability of research and evaluation to provide the critical lens needed for feedback on the effects of a society's practices, policies, and structures on itself.

What is unmistakable is that the history and role of evaluation in society and what counts as evaluation are political decisions that cannot be separated from the social justice principles guiding them (House, 2005). "Principles of social justice are used to assess whether the distribution of benefits and burdens among members of a society are appropriate, fair, and moral" (House, 2005, p. 1074). As a practice meant to improve society, evaluation is implicated in discussions about which societal and cultural values and principles of justice will prevail and which ones will get subverted or ignored altogether. Although attention to context and the inclusion of stakeholder views in evaluation practice have long been considered a core component of evaluation in

NEW DIRECTIONS FOR EVALUATION, no. 127, Fall 2010 © Wiley Periodicals, Inc., and the American Evaluation Association. Published online in Wiley Online Library (wileyonlinelibrary.com) • DOI: 10.1002/ev.334

a democratic society, how these elements should be taken into account is a long-standing dispute among evaluators (Ryan & Cousins, 2009; Shaw, Greene, & Mark, 2006). For example, even though the inclusion of stakeholder perspectives is a guiding principle for evaluators, what this means can involve seeking out the responses of stakeholders on a survey instrument, on the one hand, or engagement of diverse stakeholders in the design of the evaluation, on the other. Both count as involvement but are likely to have very different effects on evaluation practice and results. The evaluation approaches used, therefore, have important consequences for the kind of society stakeholders and citizens seek to maintain or transform (Mathison, 2009; Schwandt, 2002). Many theorists believe that it is only by examining and critically assessing how knowledge is produced and reproduced in society, such as through evaluation practice, that we can better reflect on and imagine new social configurations and relations (Dant, 2003). A critical social theory approach is one way to integrate a values and social justice lens in evaluation while also assessing the way evaluation practice shapes social relationships in a democratic society.

Critical Social Theory

Critical theory is a pedagogical approach that employs a systematic and historical critique of social and cultural formations and practices in a way that fosters citizens' abilities to evaluate and alter them. Jordan and Yeomans (1995) argue that such an approach "is derived from Gramsci's (1974) notion that social relations are always essentially pedagogical in nature" (p. 390) and therefore altering any social relationship needs to occur through that relationship itself. Central to a critical theory argument is that systems like capitalism produce knowledge in such a way as to obscure their oppressive consequences. Unjust practices reflecting economic, cultural, and political systems, therefore, do not manifest themselves in straightforward ways but become distorted and hidden over time within contextually and culturally embedded practices. People position themselves in practices according to ways they have "learned" to see their rightful position. Therefore, critical theorists seek to develop pedagogical approaches that help participants unlearn harmful conceptions of self and others, while actively participating in constructing new forms of knowledge, including those of justice.

> Critical theory is concerned with mediating the ideals of philosophy (which includes such notions as "freedom," "equality," "justice," and "reconciliation") and society's prevailing practices and underlying tendencies. What makes critical theory "critical," indeed, is its refusal to yield unilaterally to either one. (Sherman, 2003, p. 188)

The foundational assumption guiding critical social theory is that knowledge generation can provide the basis for social transformation, but

NEW DIRECTIONS FOR EVALUATION • DOI: 10.1002/ev

it requires a different kind of knowledge than traditionally endorsed by social scientists and a different kind of relationship between social scientists and citizens (Calhoun & Karaganis, 2001; Rasmussen, 1996). Although what this means varies, the core concept is that social science practices themselves cannot simply be regarded as the means to an end, but must themselves be openly scrutinized to understand better their effects on the structures and practices under investigation. In other words, what differentiates a critical social theory from other theories guiding social science is skepticism that theory and practice serve each other well when kept separate, that is, when one is seen as the explanation for the other. How people view the world, make sense of it, and act on it, are effects of theory and practice, historical and local, and need to be examined in ways that uncover the historical and local conditions for current practices in order to improve them.

Evaluation as Social Critique

At the center of a critical theory approach is the notion of critique and who in society should serve as a social critic. Although the social critic is often thought of as a person who unwelcomingly shares his or her opinion whenever given the chance, the kind of critique envisioned by critical theorists is not of this sort. In the German philosophical tradition, "'critique' means not simply criticism, but rather a deep examination of the conditions under which any particular form of thinking could operate" (Calhoun & Karaganis, 2001, p. 180). Critical theorists conceive of a particular kind of citizen in society, one who works alongside evaluators and researchers in the development of a shared awareness and critique of the failures of political and economic systems to self-assess and change (Dant, 2003), what Westheimer and Kahne (2004) call a "justice-oriented citizen." Furthermore, this citizen is not a disinterested, detached, and dispassionate social scientist, but is a person, social scientist or citizen, who is connected to and cares deeply about the issues he or she seeks to change (Waltzer, 1987). What is needed for a democracy to thrive is a way to expand this conception of citizen among citizens, rather than assuming that only some people should carry forth this social responsibility. "When only a few decide social policy, an aristocracy, plutocracy, or technocracy exists, depending on whether talent, money, or expertise is the source of authority" (House & Howe, 1999, p. 11). A critical theory approach seeks ways to put that authority in the hands of people.

The Chapters in This Issue

To develop a better understanding of the challenges of and opportunities for a critical theory evaluation, this *New Directions for Evaluation* issue focuses on issues, examples, and processes relevant to the carrying out of evaluation primarily, and secondarily to an analysis of how critical social theory informed, or might have informed, those processes. The introductory and concluding chapters provide different perspectives and commentaries for understanding critical theory and its role in and effect on evaluation practice.

Each of the authors in this issue have considered what a critical theory lens might offer evaluation practice. Although coming from a variety of disciplines and discussing different kinds of evaluation practice, they share a concern for social justice and the belief that evaluation can further a social justice agenda. As such, each chapter advances our understanding of how evaluation practice or theory affects or potentially affects "how the good and bad things in life . . . [become] distributed among the members of a human society" (Miller, 1999, p. 1).

In the introductory chapter, Melissa Freeman and Erika França S. Vasconcelos present an overview of critical theory's history and key tenets. Then, using critical pedagogy as an example, they describe the kinds of issues facing evaluators as they bring together four of the subtheories that comprise a critical social theory: (1) a theory of false consciousness, (2) a theory of crisis, (3) a theory of education, and (4) a theory of transformative action. They conclude by advocating for more, not less, attention being paid to a critical theory approach in evaluation.

In Chapter 2, Barbara Hooper documents how being self-critical can illuminate how practices maintain oppressive conditions. Using the example of a formative evaluation of a residential program for individuals transitioning from prison to community, she shows how the evaluation processes were both consistent and inconsistent with the critical theory framework that guided them. Her narrative account documents well the potential and challenge of integrating critical theory principles into evaluation practice.

In Chapter 3, Sarah Zeller-Berkman highlights another way that evaluation practice can inadvertently oppress the very people it is seeking to benefit. Using a critical theory lens, she examines how a prominent theory of change guiding the youth-development field reinforces a transmission orientation where youth are seen as recipients of services rather than valued participants in a transformative agenda benefiting them and their communities. Zeller-Berkman shows the way evaluation designs serving the field take up and reproduce this transmissive view rather than challenge it.

In Chapter 4, Melissa Freeman, Judith Preissle, and Steven Havick draw from the evaluation of the implementation of a youth leadership camp to examine the tensions created between wanting to be responsive and wanting to intervene in the implementation process critically. They conclude by arguing that incorporating dialogue and moral discourse in evaluation may be one way to help balance evaluators' obligations to promote the well-being of society with responsibilities to clients and other stakeholders.

In Chapter 5, Christina Segerholm draws on her extensive critique of educational policy to illustrate its reliance on outcomes-based measures and offers an alternative view for educational assessment that brings together hermeneutic and critical theory concepts and practices.

NEW DIRECTIONS FOR EVALUATION • DOI: 10.1002/ev

In Chapter 6, George W. Noblit and Michelle Jay document how a critical race theory perspective can illuminate the way a team of evaluators constructed a counternarrative of school reform while working with James Comer's School Development Program.

In the concluding chapter, Linda Mabry examines how evaluation practice looks to principles and practices offered by critical social theory, first in relation to its development as a profession, and then as distinguished from postmodern approaches to evaluation.

How we evaluate reflects how we conceptualize this practice in, and for, society. The promise of critical theory is its assumption that citizens have the capacity to envision a different society; one that rejects social structures that maintain oppressive practices and looks beyond individual gains to conceive of new relationships between self and others (Fay, 1987). A consideration for a critical theory evaluation seems especially relevant today as our society is undergoing rapid economic and environmental transformations and our democratic processes are being threatened as more and more authoritative and restrictive policies are put into place under a guise of imminent threat by terrorism and an uncertain future. The intent of this issue is to show the relevance of critical social theory for evaluation as a pedagogical approach that fosters critical dialogue for the purpose of developing more socially just practices and social relations among people involved or affected by the programs being evaluated.

Note

Two years ago, my good friend Cheryl MacNeil and I were drinking coffee and chatting about the idea of doing a *New Directions for Evaluation* issue on critical social theory and evaluation practice. Although she did not pursue the project with me, our initial venture into organizing the topic and our work together over the years have deeply influenced my thinking and understanding of this theoretical approach, so it is by acknowledging her presence that I introduce this issue.

References

Calhoun, C., & Karaganis, J. (2001). Critical theory. In G. Ritzer & B. Smart (Eds.), *Handbook of social theory* (pp. 179–200). Thousand Oaks, CA: Sage.

Dant, T. (2003). *Critical social theory: Culture, society and critique.* Thousand Oaks, CA: Sage.

Fay, B. (1987). *Critical social science: Liberation and its limits.* Ithaca, NY: Cornell University Press.

House, E. R. (2005). Qualitative evaluation and changing social policy. In N. K. Denzin & Y. S. Lincoln (Eds.), *The Sage handbook of qualitative research* (3rd ed., pp. 1069–1081). Thousand Oaks, CA: Sage.

House, E. R., & Howe, K. R. (1999). *Values in evaluation and social research.* Thousand Oaks, CA: Sage.

Jordan, S., & Yeomans, D. (1995). Critical ethnography: Problems of contemporary theory and practice. *British Journal of Sociology of Education, 16*(3), 389–408.

Mathison, S. (2009). Serving the public interest through educational evaluation: Salvaging democracy by rejecting neo-liberalism. In K. E. Ryan & J. B. Cousins (Eds.), *The Sage international handbook of educational evaluation* (pp. 525–538). Thousand Oaks, CA: Sage.

Merton, R. K., & Lerner, D. (1951). Social scientists and research policy. In D. Lerner & H. D. Lasswell (Eds.), *The policy sciences: Recent developments in scope and method* (pp. 282–363). Stanford, CA: Stanford University Press.

Miller, D. (1999). *Principles of social justice.* Cambridge, MA: Harvard University Press.

Rasmussen, D. M. (1996). Critical theory and philosophy. In D. M. Rasmussen (Ed.), *Handbook of critical theory* (pp. 11–38). Cambridge, MA: Blackwell.

Ryan, K. E., & Cousins, J. B. (Eds.). (2009). *The Sage international handbook of educational evaluation.* Thousand Oaks, CA: Sage.

Schwandt, T. A. (2002). *Evaluation practice reconsidered.* New York: Peter Lang.

Shaw, I., Greene, J. C., & Mark, M. M. (Eds.). (2006). *The Sage handbook of evaluation.* Thousand Oaks, CA: Sage.

Sherman, D. (2003). Critical theory. In R. C. Solomon & D. Sherman (Eds.), *The Blackwell guide to continental philosophy* (pp. 188–218). Malden, MA: Blackwell.

Waltzer, M. (1987). *Interpretation and social criticism.* Cambridge, MA: Harvard University Press.

Westheimer, J., & Kahne, J. (2004). What kind of citizen? The politics of education for democracy. *American Educational Research Journal, 41*(2), 237–269.

Melissa Freeman
Editor

MELISSA FREEMAN is associate professor of qualitative research methodologies in the College of Education at the University of Georgia; her research focuses on critical, hermeneutic, and relational approaches to educational research and evaluation.

Freeman, M., & Vasconcelos, E.F.S. (2010). Critical social theory: Core tenets, inherent issues. In M. Freeman (Ed.), *Critical social theory and evaluation practice. New Directions for Evaluation, 127*, 7–19.

1

Critical Social Theory: Core Tenets, Inherent Issues

Melissa Freeman, Erika França S. Vasconcelos

Abstract

This chapter outlines the core tenets of critical social theory and describes inherent issues facing evaluators conducting critical theory evaluation. Using critical pedagogy as an example, the authors describe the issues facing evaluators by developing four of the subtheories that comprise a critical social theory: (a) a theory of false consciousness, (b) a theory of crisis, (c) a theory of education, and (d) a theory of transformative action. They conclude by advocating for more, not less, attention being paid to a critical theory approach in evaluation. © Wiley Periodicals, Inc., and the American Evaluation Association.

C ritical social theorists are critical of what they see as pervasive inequalities and injustices in everyday social relationships and arrangements. They view society as a human construction in need of reconstruction. A "critical social theory" is both the process and the outcome of a transformational agenda and brings together multiple beliefs about human understanding and misunderstanding, the nature of change, and the role of critique and education in society. It is an evaluative as well as a political activity that involves assessing how things are in order to transform them into what they ought to be. Because critical social theory advocates for change, it has often been portrayed as a deterministic approach seeking a desired emancipatory outcome (Lather, 1986). Our primary objective in this

NEW DIRECTIONS FOR EVALUATION, no. 127, Fall 2010 © Wiley Periodicals, Inc., and the American Evaluation Association. Published online in Wiley Online Library (wileyonlinelibrary.com) • DOI: 10.1002/ev.335

chapter is to supplant that perception with another: A desired outcome can only be established in the context of a specific social group seeking to resolve a specific issue.

We conceive of critical theory as a participatory approach that engages constituents or stakeholders in a reflective and critical reassessment of the relationship between overarching social, economic, or political systems, such as capitalism or accountabilism, and everyday practices. Central to a critical theory argument is that systems like capitalism produce knowledge in such a way as to obscure their oppressive consequences. Unjust practices and arrangements, therefore, do not manifest themselves in straightforward ways but become distorted and hidden over time within contextually and culturally embedded practices (Dant, 2003). Critical social theory offers a historical framework that both challenges the theoretical or ideological underpinnings of everyday practice and uses stakeholder perspectives of and experiences with those practices to develop new ways of conceiving of their meaning and purpose in society (Lather, 1986).

In other words, critical theory is the label for a group of participatory, pedagogical, and action-oriented theories that advocate for a certain kind of evaluation or inquiry approach. *Participatory* because critical theorists cannot know beforehand how a social system has become enmeshed in a particular context and practice, nor can they know what forms of oppression or injustices are present without engaging the stakeholders themselves in identifying and naming those injustices. *Pedagogical* because critical theorists believe that the process of assessing practices from a critical perspective involves learning new ways of perceiving people's roles and locations in the perpetuation and resistance of oppressive structures. *Action oriented* because critical social theorists stress that the development of new understanding is contingent on changes in practice and material conditions, and cannot rely on rhetoric alone. Furthermore, critical theorists maintain that critical theory is an integral part of building and sustaining a more just society, one in which all members of that society feel empowered to carry out their practices in ways that foster democratic and empowering processes and outcomes, while continuously monitoring those processes and outcomes for evidence of social injustices.

Although involving analyses of local and historical particularities, critical social theories share several assumptions and approaches. We provide an overview of critical social theory's core principles and concerns, describe how we think it can benefit evaluation practice and society, and conclude by delineating some key issues facing critical social theory evaluators.

Critical Social Theory

Critical social theory has a complex and multifaceted history that is usually traced back to the 1920s and 1930s in the work of theorists associated with the Institute for Social Research in Frankfurt, Germany. Commonly known as the Frankfurt School, the institute was originally established and funded by Felix Weil, an Argentinean political scientist interested in the study of socialism and Marxism. Before long, however, social, economic, and political conditions, especially in relation to the rise of fascism in various parts of the world, altered the focus of Frankfurt School theorists away from orthodox Marxism to a more varied perspective on theory and culture (Dant, 2003; Rasmussen, 1996). Although varied in terms of specific concerns, theoretical constructs, and disciplinary applications, critical social theories share several core principles. Historically, the primary function of critical theory is the establishment of a sustained critique of all social formations, whether cultural, economic, or political, with an eye to preventing any one form from taking control of the world in a way that is antidemocratic, unjust, exploitative, or oppressive (Dant, 2003; Sherman, 2003).

In general, critical social theorists posit a constitutional relationship between the structures of a society and its members, where everyone is affected, albeit in different ways and to different degrees (Dant, 2003). Connected to this is a belief that the knowledge generated by oppressive systems has become so embedded in everyday practices that it is a distortion and misrepresentation of human experiences and desires. For example, critical theorists believe that modern societies perpetuate oppressive structures by promoting one dominant way of thinking in the form of "instrumental reason" (Dant, 2003, p. 160), which obscures and excludes the values, desires, and experiences of social members. The solution, according to critical social theorists, is to engage in some form of ideology critique that is both critically reflective of people's roles and experiences in everyday practice and historically grounded in an analysis of how those practices have been developed and supported within modern systems (Calhoun & Karaganis, 2001). This approach is considered necessary because one of the effects obscuring the relationship humans have with dominant structures is that inequalities are taken to be natural occurrences, and so, embedded in the notion of critique is an antioppressive pedagogy oriented to social change. Therefore, critique is emancipatory in that it entails the capability to explore, without constraints, alternative meanings and realities (Dant, 2003).

Furthermore, critical social theorists reject the belief that theory and practice are separate forms of human activity, and view both as intrinsically embodied in praxis, in the way humans act out their theoretical versions of the world. In other words, conversations that tie theory and practice together go beyond the immediate concerns individuals may have to involve a critical appraisal of the values, commitments, visions, and principles they have about their practices, their roles in society, and so on, as well as to a consideration of how their practices enable or hamper reaching those objectives (Schwandt, 2005). A common criticism of critical theory is that it pushes toward a predetermined outcome for these conversations; however, critical theory is primarily a theory of practice that is shaped through its interaction with others regarding that practice.

NEW DIRECTIONS FOR EVALUATION • DOI: 10.1002/ev

Modernist and Postmodernist Variations

Although change-oriented and antioppressive in vision, critical social theories differ. One point of contrast occurs between a modernist perspective associated with the Frankfurt School, which relies on the recovery of a critical form of reason as the solution to human emancipation from domination, and a postmodernist perspective exemplified in the work of Michel Foucault, which challenges the effectiveness of such a recovery (Leonard, 1990). Both views stress that even though historically affected, oppressive and emancipatory knowledges must be understood within local and contextually specific practices (Leonard, 1990). Both also assert that language itself carries forth its own history of meaning; thus any account, local or otherwise, needs to be scrutinized for its multiple meanings.

Where they differ, however, is in their overall view of society and the role they bestow to theory in the service of emancipation. For example, even while believing that the intersection of theory and practice occurs in local contexts, Frankfurt School theorists rely on a grand theory of how society changes (in an evolutionary progression) and the necessary means for its evolution toward democracy (through critical rational means) (Leonard, 1990). In their view, enlightenment is achieved through self-knowledge and the ability of oppressed people to recover a genuine narrative of their history (Fay, 1987). Foucaultian theorists, on the other hand, reject evolutionary progressive visions of society as well as the belief that reason is ultimately just (Leonard, 1990). Casting aside a focus on structures of knowledge, they advocate for a genealogical approach that traces the way knowledge and power are produced in discursive formations (Leonard, 1990).

At its extremes, the first view asserts that there is no possibility of emancipation for individuals without structural reorganization, whereas the second wishes to free the individual from the constraints of all structures, discursive or physical. In practice, critical social theorists tend to lean more toward one or the other, but often draw on components of each perspective. For example, multiple modernist perspectives, while still supporting enlightenment ideals of social progress, draw on art, performance, or narrative as an alternative to rational thinking (Conquergood, 2006; Foley, 2002; Foley & Valenzuela, 2005).

Critical Social Theory Evaluation

Conducting critical theory evaluation means taking both a value-committed and value-critical stance (Schwandt, 1997) and advocating for "political democratic ideals" (Greene, 2006, p. 118) while engaging critically with stakeholders about the social values embedded in the practice or issue under scrutiny. Our view is that values are an integral part of what evaluators must deal with, what they bring with them, and what they strive to articulate in their work (Becker, 1967). However, here we are not arguing for taking the side of the rich or the poor, the powerful or the powerless. Instead we are arguing for taking the side of social justice, and what that means and involves is part of what the inquiry process must both determine and then use as the basis for action. Advocating for democratic ideals does not mean that the evaluator has a predetermined solution for the problems or oppressions articulated by the stakeholders. What it does mean, however, is that critical theory evaluation offers a variety of pedagogical processes that seek to foster the development of a more socially just society, whether by strengthening social capital through citizen deliberation (MacNeil, 2002) or dialoguing about the moral import of a practice (Schwandt, 1989).

Critical theorists seek to engage stakeholders who may not hold similar values or social positions within a program, practice, or community in ways that foster the transformation of individual understandings and adherences to taken-for-granted beliefs about self and others, while developing a commitment to collective action based on the transformative knowledge generated by the group's interactions (Lather, 1986; Leonardo, 2004). Depending on the context and expressed needs, this engagement can take on multiple forms. The evaluator becomes researcher, facilitator, negotiator, educator, learner, change agent, and critic (Everitt, 1996; MacNeil, 2005).

In other words, critical social theory and critical evaluation share certain assumptions about the promise and role of social inquiry in society. Advocates of both:

- believe that society can be improved, or altered, through education and intervention and that all social practices are interventions, whether they claim neutrality or advocate from a particular stance
- are constrained as well as supported by local contexts, knowledge, interests, and needs
- stress the inclusion of diverse perspectives and interests
- emphasize that the process of the inquiry is just as important as the result, and that it should sustain and develop democratic values and decision-making processes whenever possible
- are self-critical and self-reflective about how their practices are implicated in maintaining or creating oppressive structures and relationships
- assert that local values determining merit and worth need to be accounted for but that their revision or transformation is likely to be one effect or one intended objective of the inquiry
- locate the validity of the inquiry in its capacity to effect change, thus seeking catalytic validity (Lather, 1986) as a central determination of the success or quality of the inquiry

Inherent Issues for Critical Theory Evaluators

Embedded in all critical social theories are four interrelated theories (Fay, 1987, pp. 31–32), which we paraphrase in our own words: (a) a theory of false consciousness, which explains the nature and process through which social members' values and beliefs become obscured and distorted by dominant ideologies, (b) a theory of crisis, which locates and describes the source and nature of the oppression in question, (c) a theory of education, which accounts for the conditions and processes necessary for the enlightenment or alternative visions to surface, and (d) a theory of transformative action, which details the kinds of actions and alterations needed to resolve the identified crisis. Enlightenment and emancipatory action are developed by people within a particular sociohistoric context for a specific purpose, and so the value and success of the purpose, process, and structure of a critical theory relies on its catalytic validity, its ability to empower stakeholders to alter their oppressed situation (Lather, 1986; Leonard, 1990).

What does it mean to change our understanding of how society works and how does this presumably new understanding contribute to changing society? If anything has clearly emerged from critical social theory's history, it is that a transformational agenda takes multiple shapes and targets different needs and interests, and, as such, its variability of means and ends is an issue that every critical theorist inherits and must account for. Drawing on Fay's (1987) four subtheories and Freire's (1970/1993) critical pedagogy as examples of a pedagogical and participatory critical approach, we outline the inherent issues (Smith, 2008) facing critical social theorist evaluators. Subsequent chapters provide examples of how some of these issues might play out in practice. The broad question here is: What fundamental issues are involved in a critical approach?

A theory of false consciousness. Critical pedagogy originated with the publication of Freire's (1970/1993) *Pedagogy of the Oppressed*, arguably the most important educator in the last half of the 20th century (Kohl, 1997). In the past four decades, the field has undergone many transformations as critical pedagogues have deployed new strategies to confront changing social and historical contexts and to account for the perspectives and considerations of the participants in those contexts. It is thus unsurprising that critical pedagogy is not a unitary set of texts, beliefs, convictions, or assumptions, and some scholars may prefer the plural, *critical pedagogies* (Norton & Toohey, 2004, p. 2). Nevertheless, these theories share a desire to offer people tools for the critical and creative analysis of their own circumstances (Wallace, 2003). People in different educational and community contexts are encouraged to examine the sociopolitical, economic, and historical realities that shape their lives, in order to make new meanings and develop cultural practices that are critical, transformative, and liberatory.

One of the central beliefs driving critical theory and critical pedagogy is that reeducation is required because the oppressed "have internalized the values, beliefs, and even world view of their oppressors . . . [and] willingly cooperate with those who oppress them in maintaining those social practices that result in their oppression" (Fay, 1987, p. 107). This internalized process, commonly known as *false consciousness*, raises several issues for the critical evaluator, the first being how to define false consciousness in order to address it.

Freire believed that false consciousness should not be equated with ignorance or a deficiency in individuals. A belief in ignorance promotes what Freire (1970/1993) termed "banking education" (p. 53), which he equates with the use of education as an instrument of oppression. Banking education occurs when teachers as certified possessors of legitimized knowledge perceive learners as empty containers that need to be filled with preestablished bodies of knowledge. Students', and other learners', actions are limited to receiving, filling, and storing deposits of information, which are often disconnected from their social realities.

To break with the top-down precedent of banking education, Freire argued for the practice of a political education grounded in an emancipatory pedagogy. For Freire, a critical, liberatory pedagogy emphasizes the development of *conscientização*, often translated from Portuguese as *critical consciousness* or *consciousness-making*. Developing critical consciousness entails assessing the system of social institutions, social traditions, and social relations that create and maintain conditions of oppression, while also recognizing and acknowledging one's role in that system. The learner should be able to situate him- or herself in his or her own historicity, for example, to grasp the class, race, and gender aspects of education and social formation and to understand the complexity of the relations that have produced this situation (Aronowitz, 1998, p. 14). Critical consciousness enables the oppressed to see themselves as active subjects, rather than passive objects that are acted upon. Critical consciousness is the beginning point of liberatory praxis, configured as an ongoing, reflective approach to taking action.

Although false consciousness can be thought of as "social life . . . systematically distorted by social forces" (Wood, 1988, p. 358), it is often cast as a stagnant, uncritical, and uneducated view of the world held by some individuals and not others, rather than as a complex social phenomenon affecting all people, albeit in different ways. In Freire's (1970/1993) view, everyone, the oppressors as well as the oppressed, are appropriate subjects for emancipation. The goal in his democratic approach is a drive toward reconciliation. Reconciliation involves the joint recognition by individuals who are positioned in unequal relation with each other, such as teachers–students, staff–clients, doctor–patient, of the way they have both been thus positioned by systems of oppression. The solution to resolving the teacher–student contradiction lies in both parties understanding their interdependent, often unintended, contributions to the maintenance of the oppressive situation. For transformation to occur for anyone, transformation has to occur for all. Power and powerlessness sustain each other, and in the tensions created in that interdependency are the possibilities for new relationships and new configurations of arrangements (Fay, 1987).

Critical social theorists hold different opinions about how best to address false consciousness. If false conciousness is understood as an individual condition, the success or failure of its release (i.e., the solution) is dependent upon individual ability, desire, or motivation. Understanding false conciousness as a phenomenon created within society brings about its own challenges in terms of structural reorganization (Augoustinos, 1999). Therefore, understanding the relationship between false consciousness and emancipation is a core issue for evaluators considering a critical approach.

A theory of crisis. Because the complex relationship between false consciousness and reconciliation involves understanding how the effects of power create divided and conflicted relationships among stakeholders, it follows that the identification of a genuine crisis whose resolution supports and enables reconciliation will not be easy. The crises most likely to be first considered are themselves most apt to have been manufactured by systems of oppression. These are the ones that, although seeming to benefit underprivileged or other marginalized groups, serve to maintain structures that create systems where group interests are pitted against each other, hiding the reality of people's joint dehumanization. Crises such as "achievement gaps" or "welfare mothers" contribute to maintaining a system in which people who are so identified are seen as problems in relation to people who are not, rather than considering that a system that contributes to these effects is in need of reconfiguration. An issue facing evaluators is how to affirm and recognize the importance these manufactured crises play in people's lives while moving the conversation to one of understanding how society has created these issues.

One of the fundamental issues of a participatory-oriented critical theory is its reliance on the willingness and interest of humans to reflect on and dialogue about their own practice. People are often inundated with calls for change, making this kind of profound inquiry likely to be resisted. The critical evaluator has to work within the reality of this resistance, understand the history of the practice and people involved, and willingly listen to multiple contradictory perceptions of what ought to be the purpose of the evaluation, its process, and outcome. Learning and listening are a crucial part of this process, as the evaluator seeks to understand the lived details of the people connected to the practice or program under scrutiny. In such a way, mutual trust is built from a shared horizon of possible perspectives, and the impetus for commitment and change becomes the necessary signal that more critical work can begin.

A commitment to active engagement and learning is necessary so that the dialogue that follows encourages everyone to listen and learn as much as possible about the apparent issues, how these issues are thought to have come about, how they are being expressed, and by whom. In this way, uncovering the values, assumptions, contradictions, and tensions becomes a major part of the evaluative process, a process that assists in understanding the crisis of which these issues are a symptom. Within the perceptions of those involved lie differing beliefs about the relationship of structures to agency, the nature of understanding and change, or the role of teaching and learning. What the program or practice means to the people involved, what effect, if any, it has on their lives, are the kernels of its importance and effect on people, and the building blocks of a critical theory (Kushner, 2000).

NEW DIRECTIONS FOR EVALUATION • DOI: 10.1002/ev

A theory of education. Education, here, is conceived of in its broadest sense, as the teaching and learning that takes place in any social group, not just formal schooling. For Freire (1970/1993), the cornerstone of his critical pedagogy was dialogue, whether it occurred in formal or informal social gatherings. Freire (1970/1993, 1998a) believed that true dialogue is infused with love for the world and for people, humility, faith in humankind, and hope for positive change. Love is commitment to others and to the cause of liberation (Freire, 1970/1993, p. 70). This kind of dialogue involves a commitment to seeing others as having something to teach us and in turn showing those others that we have faith in our interconnected ability to remake the world.

In this conception of education, face-to-face dialogue between people who hold different conceptions of the world or practice under scrutiny is crucial. Dialogue becomes the basis within which a critical and problem-posing discourse is acquired and practiced. The critical educator committed to reconciliation challenges the learners with whom she communicates by practicing problem-posing education (Freire, 1970/1993). Problem-posing education, or "education as the practice of freedom" (hooks, 1994), promotes practices that encourage people to perceive critically the way they exist in the world and see the world not as a static reality, but as a reality in process, in transformation. The point of departure must be the "here and now"—the situation within which they are submerged, from which they emerge, and in which they can intervene. Through problem-posing dialogue, the stakeholders begin to understand why they must comprehend the effects society has had on the creation of their current situation in order to begin to break free of that hold and articulate new configurations for themselves and their practice. The educator or evaluator becomes facilitator and participant of this dialogic process, sometimes taking on multiple roles, such as Clayson et al. (2002) did in a multicultural setting, as they acted as "interpreters, translators, mediators, and storytellers" (p. 35), each role advancing negotiation and democratizing processes in important ways.

There is a fragile line between critical education and indoctrination into criticality that must be attended to (Burbules & Berk, 1999). One criticism of critical pedagogy is its inability to move out of a modernist, progressive view of education as the means to emancipation—an emancipation guided by the vision of a possible utopia (Biesta, 1998). Biesta (1998) provides one example of an alternative way of thinking of emancipation through education. Rather than view education as a process of replacing distortions with an ideal democratic society, he suggests that educators shed all pretense of knowing the critical route to emancipation. In other words, Biesta asserts that critical pedagogy's weakness is its taken-for-granted acceptance of its own authority. He argues instead for a renewal of human interaction itself, interactions that are characteristically unpredictable, contradictory, and non-teleological. By questioning and dialoguing, stakeholders find out about themselves and their hopes and beliefs, as they work to construct and reconstruct a possible version of their social world (Schwandt, 2002).

NEW DIRECTIONS FOR EVALUATION • DOI: 10.1002/ev

Developing a critical process does not require consensus of perspective and procedure (Freire, 1998b; 2005); it does require trust in each other's desire to learn and inquire together, which involves risk and exposure and humility (Freire, 2005), as well as pride. Mutual trust is invited at the onset, when the evaluator describes a critical theory approach with honesty about what it entails from people in terms of time, commitment, and the lack of a clear process. Mutual trust, and thus critical work, however, might not be a feasible goal in some settings or in settings where the evaluator has not already established a long-term working partnership (Mathison, 1994). These issues all become part of the overall judgment call of critical theory evaluators.

A theory of transformative action. As mentioned previously, critical theory is not a theory that is imposed on a process, but a process that puts into practice a multiplicity of theories in the creation of transformative action. A critical approach does not seek to offer or impose solutions because "part of the solution can be found in how the problem is addressed in the first place" (Leonardo, 2004, p. 13). In other words, people's awareness of their complicity or oppressive behavior has to accompany their response to it; this can only happen simultaneously in practice. The validity of the process is found in the success of the transformative or emancipatory action. But what is emancipation? How is it achieved? Is it an individual transformation or a social one? Fay (1987) has criticized critical social theory for its emphasis on the enlightenment of individuals at the expense of understanding its relevance for "mass social action" (p. 108).

Evaluators' views of emancipation are shaped by the evaluation practice and context, and draw on their understandings about false consciousness and education. Conceptualizing alternative ways of bringing about emancipatory outcomes and remaining open to what emancipation might look like, while simultaneously working for its achievement, are challenges facing the critical evaluator. We believe that the ability to conceptualize these overlapping and mutually dependent perspectives is essential if the critical social theory evaluator is going to be successful at effectively communicating to a variety of stakeholders what participation and commitment to a critical theory evaluation entails.

The Road Ahead

Greene (2001) and Mertens (2001) argued for a renewed commitment to examine and reconsider the role of evaluation in society, especially in regards to its potential to uncover and overturn oppressive social practices. Furthermore, House (1993, 2005) has long argued that a condition plaguing evaluation is that it has a tendency to be taken up by and to reflect the problems of modern society, rather than to act as its arbiter. House advocated for principles of inclusion, dialogue, deliberation, and social justice as central to evaluation practice and as one way to prevent evaluation from serving the status quo, while also benefiting society. For House and others, the link between social justice and evaluation seems a natural fit, as both are intended to assist in improving society.

To be certain, other evaluation models are directed at engaging stakeholders in deliberation and transformational narratives in order to move social organizations toward more empowering or socially just practices. There is, however, not a single critical approach. Quite the contrary, we see our work drawing from multiple evaluation models, such as responsive, participatory, and deliberative democratic, as well as valuing the contribution of an explicit critical theory perspective. Our aim is to shed some light on a tradition that has received its share of criticisms in a way that fosters growth and understanding of its potential for evaluation. Although many of the criticisms it has garnered, such as being too theoretical and distant from the lives of real people (Lather, 1986), too rhetorical as opposed to action oriented (Anderson, 1989), too disempowering as opposed to empowering (Ellsworth, 1989), and lacking its own self-awareness and critique (Gore, 1992, 1993), are, in some cases, warranted, this does not justify abandoning a critical theory agenda. Rather, it suggests a need for more, not less, examination of its strengths and weaknesses; engaging in, rather than retreating from, questioning; and considering how critical theory evaluation can benefit the field of evaluation, the programs we serve, and society.

Critical theory offers a theoretical lens for assessing the relationships individuals have with the social structures and institutional practices they work within and encounter every day. It offers a way to understand better the effect these social structures have on people's beliefs, ideologies, actions, interactions, and communicative practices, while also generating insight into processes that resist, challenge, or reshape dominant forms of thinking and acting. Central to a critical theory approach is maintaining a continuous investigation of the connections between theory and practice so that the two are enmeshed and become one (Schwandt, 2005). Understanding the conditions that support or impede critical theory evaluation provides the evaluation community with a clearer perspective on its use in evaluation and contributes to broader conversations about evaluation and evaluation's role in society.

Acknowledgment

We would like to thank Judith Preissle for her valuable editorial suggestions on an earlier version of this chapter.

References

Anderson, G. L. (1989). Critical ethnography in education: Origins, current status, and new directions. *Review of Educational Research, 59*(3), 249–270.

Aronowitz, S. (1998). Introduction. In P. Freire (Ed.), *Pedagogy of freedom: Ethics, democracy, and civic courage* (pp. 1–19). Lanham, MD: Rowman & Littlefield.

Augoustinos, M. (1999). Ideology, false consciousness and psychology. *Theory & Psychology, 9*(3), 295–312.

Becker, H. S. (1967). Whose side are we on? *Social Problems, 14*(3), 239–247.

Biesta, G.J.J. (1998). Say you want a revolution . . . Suggestions for the impossible future of critical pedagogy. *Educational Theory, 48*(4), 499–510.

Burbules, N. C., & Berk, R. (1999). Critical thinking and critical pedagogy: Relations, differences, and limits. In T. S. Popkewitz & L. Fendler (Eds.), *Critical theories in education: Changing terrains of knowledge and politics* (pp. 45–66). New York: Routledge.

Calhoun, C., & Karaganis, J. (2001). Critical theory. In G. Ritzer and B. Smart (Eds.), *Handbook of social theory* (pp. 179–200). Thousand Oaks, CA: Sage.

Clayson, Z. C., Castañeda, X., Sanchez, E., & Brindis, C. (2002). Unequal power—Changing landscapes: Negotiations between evaluation stakeholders in Latino communities. *The American Journal of Evaluation, 23*(1), 33–44.

Conquergood, D. (2006). Rethinking ethnography: Towards a critical cultural politics. In D. S. Madison & J. Hamera (Eds.), *The Sage handbook of performance studies* (pp. 351–365). Thousand Oaks, CA: Sage.

Dant, T. (2003). *Critical social theory: Culture, society and critique.* Thousand Oaks, CA: Sage.

Ellsworth, M. (1989). Why doesn't this feel empowering? Working through the repressive myths of critical pedagogy. *Harvard Educational Review, 59,* 297–324.

Everitt, A. (1996). Developing critical evaluation. *Evaluation, 2*(2), 173–188.

Fay, B. (1987). *Critical social science: Liberation and its limits.* Ithaca, NY: Cornell University Press.

Foley, D. E. (2002). Critical ethnography: The reflexive turn. *Qualitative Studies in Education, 15*(5), 469–490.

Foley, D. E., & Valenzuela, A. (2005). Critical ethnography: The politics of collaboration. In N. K. Denzin & Y. S. Lincoln (Eds.), *The Sage handbook of qualitative research* (pp. 217–234). Thousand Oaks, CA: Sage.

Freire, P. (1993). *Pedagogy of the oppressed* (Rev. ed.). New York: Continuum. (Original work published 1970).

Freire, P. (1998a). *Pedagogy of freedom: Ethics, democracy, and civic courage.* Lanham, MD: Rowman & Littlefield.

Freire, P. (1998b). *Pedagogy of hope: Reliving Pedagogy of the Oppressed.* New York: Continuum.

Freire, P. (2005). *Teachers as cultural workers: Letters to those who dare teach.* Boulder, CO: Westview.

Gore, J. M. (1992). What can we do for you! What can "we" do for "you"? Struggling over empowerment in critical and feminist pedagogy. In C. Luke & J. M. Gore (Eds.), *Feminisms and critical pedagogy* (pp. 54–73). New York: Routledge.

Gore, J. M. (1993). *The struggle for pedagogies: Critical and feminist discourses as regimes of truth.* New York: Routledge.

Greene, J. (2006). Evaluation, democracy, and social change. In I. F. Shaw, J. Greene, & M. Mark (Eds.), *The Sage handbook of evaluation* (pp. 118–140). Thousand Oaks, CA: Sage.

Greene, J. C. (2001). Evaluation extrapolations. *American Journal of Evaluation, 22*(3), 397–402.

hooks, b. (1994). *Teaching to transgress: Education as the practice of freedom.* New York: Routledge.

House, E. R. (1993). *Professional evaluation: Social impact and political consequences.* Thousand Oaks, CA: Sage.

House, E. R. (2005). Qualitative evaluation and changing social policy. In N. K. Denzin & Y. S. Lincoln (Eds.), *The Sage handbook of qualitative research* (3rd ed., pp. 1069–1081). Thousand Oaks, CA: Sage.

Kohl, H. (1997, May 26). Paulo Freire: Liberation pedagogy. *The Nation,* p. 7.

Kushner, S. (2000). *Personalizing evaluation*. Thousand Oaks, CA: Sage.

Lather, P. (1986). Research as praxis. *Harvard Educational Review, 56*(3), 257–276.

Leonard, S. T. (1990). *Critical theory in political practice*. Princeton, NJ: Princeton University Press.

Leonardo, Z. (2004). Critical social theory and transformative knowledge: The functions of criticism in quality education. *Educational Researcher, 33*(6), 11–18.

MacNeil, C. (2002). Evaluator as steward of citizen deliberation. *American Journal of Evaluation, 23*(1), 45–54.

MacNeil, C. (2005). Critical theory evaluation. In S. Mathison (Ed.), *Encyclopedia of evaluation* (pp. 92–94). Thousand Oaks, CA: Sage.

Mathison, S. (1994). Rethinking the evaluator role: Partnerships between organizations and evaluators. *Evaluation and Program Planning, 17*(3), 299–304.

Mertens, D. M. (2001). Inclusivity and transformations: Evaluation in 2010. *American Journal of Evaluation, 22*(3), 367–374.

Norton, B., & Toohey, K. (Eds.). (2004). *Critical pedagogies and language learning*. Cambridge, UK: Cambridge University Press.

Rasmussen, D. M. (1996). Critical theory and philosophy. In D. M. Rasmussen (Ed.), *Handbook of critical theory* (pp. 11–38). Cambridge, MA: Blackwell.

Schwandt, T. A. (1989). Recapturing moral discourse in evaluation. *Educational Researcher, 18*(8), 11–35.

Schwandt, T. A. (1997). The landscape of values in evaluation: Charted terrain and unexplored territory. In D. J. Rog & D. Fournier (Eds.), *Progress and future directions in evaluation: Perspectives on theory, practice, and methods. New Directions for Evaluation, 76,* 25–39.

Schwandt, T. A. (2002). *Evaluation practice reconsidered*. New York: Peter Lang.

Schwandt, T. A. (2005). The centrality of practice to evaluation. *American Journal of Evaluation, 26*(1), 95–105.

Sherman, D. (2003). Critical theory. In R. C. Solomon & D. Sherman (Eds.), *The Blackwell guide to continental philosophy* (pp. 188–218). Malden, MA: Blackwell.

Smith, N. L. (2008). Fundamental issues in evaluation. In N. L. Smith & P. R. Brandon (Eds.), *Fundamental issues in evaluation* (pp. 1–23). New York: Guilford Press.

Wallace, C. (2003). *Critical reading in language education*. Basingstoke, Hampshire, UK: Palgrave Macmillan.

Wood, A. W. (1988). Ideology, false consciousness, and social illusion. In B. P. McLaughlin & A. O. Rorty (Eds.), *Perspectives on self-deception* (pp. 345–363). Berkeley: University of California Press.

MELISSA FREEMAN is associate professor of qualitative research methodologies in the College of Education at the University of Georgia; her research focuses on critical, hermeneutic, and relational approaches to educational research and evaluation.

ERIKA FRANÇA S. VASCONCELOS is a Ph.D. candidate in the Department of Language and Literacy Education at the University of Georgia; her research interests include Freirean critical/dialogic pedagogy, second/foreign language education, teacher education, critical discourse analysis, and Brazilian literature.

Hooper, B. (2010). Falling forward: Lessons learned from critical reflection on an evaluation process with a prisoner reentry program. In M. Freeman (Ed.), *Critical social theory and evaluation practice. New Directions for Evaluation, 127*, 21–34.

2

Falling Forward: Lessons Learned From Critical Reflection on an Evaluation Process With a Prisoner Reentry Program

Barbara Hooper

Abstract

A formative evaluation of life-skills learning modules with men and women in a residential prisoner reentry program where careful attention was given to voice, power, and engagement, is described and analyzed. The author reflects on the evaluation process through the critical theory lens of "being self-critical can illuminate how practices maintain oppressive conditions." Questions about whose voices remained dominant and whose power was suppressed are discussed. © Wiley Periodicals, Inc., and the American Evaluation Association.

Freeman and Vasconcelos (this issue) identified the assumptions that critical evaluators share in common with critical social theory. These include the following:

- Society can be improved or altered through education and intervention.
- Both the process and the result of inquiry should uphold democratic values and decision making.
- Diverse perspectives and voices should be included in the evaluation process.
- Practices are constrained and supported by local contexts, knowledge, interests, and needs.

NEW DIRECTIONS FOR EVALUATION, no. 127, Fall 2010 © Wiley Periodicals, Inc., and the American Evaluation Association. Published online in Wiley Online Library (wileyonlinelibrary.com) • DOI: 10.1002/ev.336

- The transformation of local practices is a likely and desired outcome of evaluation.
- The practice is validated in its capacity to elicit change.
- Being self-critical and self-reflective can illuminate how practices maintain or create oppressive structures and relationships.

In this chapter, I use the above assumption—that being self-critical can illuminate how practices maintain oppressive conditions—to examine a program-evaluation process with a community-based residential program for former prisoners transitioning to the community. Using this assumption as a lens for reflection revealed that the evaluation was ultimately both consistent and inconsistent with the beliefs of a critical evaluator. I first describe the program, then describe how each phase of the evaluation both enacted some of the above beliefs and also had elements that may have inadvertently sustained the power relationships we sought to equalize.

The Residential Program for Individuals Transitioning From Prison to the Community

Residents were admitted to the community transition program from multiple corrections facilities through an application and interview process. Individuals were eligible for the residential program if they were over the age of 18, had not been convicted of violent crimes or larceny, had demonstrated a commitment to self-improvement while in prison, and had no documented chronic persistent mental illness. Up to 13 women and 20 men could participate in the program at any given time. While in the program, residents lived in one of five homes located in neighborhoods throughout a city of approximately 500,000.

Residents were able to remain in, and graduate from, the program if they obtained employment within 2 weeks of admission, met all requirements of parole, paid a portion of monthly rent, actively participated in weekly meetings of Alcoholics Anonymous, remained substance-free, and attended nightly dinners and educational programs. Men and women participated in separate programming. On average, residents graduated from the program in 3 months. The program's staff included an executive director, an office manager who also conducted applicant interviews and made admissions decisions, a marketing and development staff, a part-time occupational therapist, and three house managers, two of whom were former graduates of the program. Two houses did not have on-site managers.

In addition to adhering to the above policies, the residents participated in community meals and life-skills education. Eating nightly dinners together was considered an important part of the overall transition program. Meals were believed to be a means for addressing social participation in a naturalized context. Community volunteers prepared meals for the men's and women's homes and shared the meal and cleanup process with the residents. These meals were mandatory for residents unless exceptional circumstances prevailed. In addition to community meals, the residents participated in evening life-skills programming, that, prior to my involvement, consisted of a series of one-session topics, such as managing finances, resume writing, legal issues, and locating housing, conducted by community volunteers and often delivered in a lecture format. Topics for life-skills programming were determined primarily by the executive director and community volunteers and coordinated by a staff member. The staff member in charge of life-skills programming had resigned a couple of months prior to my involvement. The executive director sought to reestablish and improve upon the life-skills portion of the overall transition program.

Empowering people to build life skills and participate in everyday activities as fully and effectively as possible is the focus of occupational therapy. The executive director decided that the expertise of occupational therapy was well-suited to what he envisioned for an expanded life-skills program. Therefore, as a member of the occupational therapy faculty at a nearby university, I was initially contracted by the executive director to establish a new life-skills program based in occupational therapy principles and practice. It was my belief, however, that a formative evaluation of existing needs, prior successes, and published literature was important to the program development process. I enlisted graduate students to help conduct a formative evaluation of life-skills programming, which is the process I critically reflect upon here. The graduate students were familiar with the life-skills program because they had been volunteering as facilitators. The evaluation consisted of an initial literature search, interviewing community volunteers who served on the advisory committee for the overall program, and finally interviewing multiple stakeholders about their perceptions of a successful transition from prison. The ultimate aim was to use the findings from the formative evaluation to build a new life-skills program, which functioned as a key aspect of the overall transition program.

Action!: Initial Planning Phase for Life-Skills Formative Evaluation and Program Development

Starting Assumptions

I began the formative evaluation with several assumptions consistent with critical theory. These can be categorized as assumptions about participation in everyday activities, the impact of incarceration on self-efficacy and everyday activities, and how internalized assumptions can be made explicit.

- Participation in everyday activities such as work, self-maintenance, or social relationships was not simply a matter of individuals receiving information and acquiring a skill. Rather, the activities with which one chooses to be occupied and how one interfaces with those activities reflect internalized social understandings of the self (Christiansen, 1999; McAdams, 1997). In other words, engagement in daily activities stems from deep beliefs created and reinforced within social systems. Therefore, life-skills programming would need to involve a critical pedagogy that, through questioning and dialogue, could illuminate the beliefs, assumptions, and experiences held about everyday activities that might support residents as community citizens.

- Participation in everyday activities such as self-care, work, leisure, education, care of others, and care of home and finances is a function of environmental opportunities for self-efficacy (Kielhofner, 2002; Lawton, 1982).
- Incarceration can mute self-efficacy along with other skills because prison environments afford little opportunity for self-determined daily activities, that is, the very skills individuals are expected to display immediately upon release (e.g., Austin, Irwin, & Hardyman, 2002; Haney, 2002; Travis, Solomon, & Waul, 2001).
- The muting power of the incarceration environment can become internalized by prisoners such that they can carry that system's social structures and values into their postrelease lives (Haney, 2002).
- The internalized incarceration system, beliefs about the self, and beliefs about participation in everyday activities often function on a tacit level. Individuals may, consequently, be run by their beliefs unaware (Kegan, 2000).
- Through heightened awareness, the beliefs and assumptions that guide participation can be held, examined, and hence modified if needed, making possible the adoption of new actions and habits (Cranton, 2002).

With these assumptions as my starting ground, I conducted a review of the literature and developed a conceptual framework for the life-skills program that I believed could inform its design and implementation.

Building the Conceptual Framework

The conceptual framework for the life-skills program included three pillars from three different fields of study—Life by Design, prisonization, and transformative learning. Life by Design was the name given to the developing life-skills program to convey a view of the person as having agency and efficacy. The name was derived from a body of occupational therapy research that demonstrated interventions to improve mental and physical health, overall life satisfaction, and occupational functioning among multicultural well elders and other groups (Horowitz & Chang, 2004; Jackson, Carlson, Mandel, Zemke, & Clark, 1998; Lipschutz, 2002). This research related to my initial assumptions described above about participation in everyday activities.

Prisonization is a concept from the criminal justice literature. Haney (2002) used the term to refer to the "ordinary adaptive process of institutionalization" (p. 1) in correction facilities that results in monumental psychological costs to prisoners returning to the community. Prisoners, for example, often experience a prolonged muting of self-initiative, continuous surveillance, quick enforcement of punishment for breaking rules, personal danger, exploitation, and no control over mundane activities such as when to get up, what clothes to wear, what to eat, and with whom to share living space. Many prisoners make psychological adaptations to these conditions that impede their transitions back into their communities. Their sense of internal control and self-efficacy can atrophy. They may become hypervigilant and suspicious and they may not have the skills to make decisions, organize their daily activities, or communicate effectively (Haney, 2002). The concept of prisonization related to my assumption above about the impact of incarceration on self-efficacy and everyday activities.

Transformative learning, from the field of education, is the process by which individuals become aware of, examine, and change, when needed, the hidden assumptions and beliefs that have been guiding their actions and perceptions. Modified beliefs and assumptions can result in modified actions and habits (Cranton, 1994; Dirkx, 2001; Mezirow, 2000). Transformative learning related to my assumption about the importance of heightening awareness of assumptions in order to adopt new actions, a process not addressed by scholarship around life by design or prisonization. These three concepts served as the knowledge bins from which I would draw to design and conduct the program evaluation and development.

Gleaning Initial Perspectives of the Program Committee

This formative evaluation was complicated by a pragmatic urgency on the part of staff to restart life-skills programming as soon as possible. This urgency led to a less-than-ideal situation in which I began developing the life-skills program simultaneously with beginning a formative evaluation. And owing to the urgency, I began by asking only members of the program committee (which included the executive director who had brought me in and volunteers from the community), "What are the most important areas of self-development that you feel residents need while in the program?" Their input resulted in the development of three modules in the Life by Design educational series: "Designing Your Next Job," "Designing Thoughts and Habits for Success at Work," and "Designing Healthy Leisure and Recreation." These modules were developed with the use of the Dirkx and Prenger (1997) theme-based adult learning principles. The modules were implemented with residents, while the formative evaluation process proceeded.

Looking Back on Phase I: Being Self-Critical Can Illuminate How Practices Maintain Oppressive Conditions

Initially I believed that the conceptual framework for the evaluation and the process for the learning modules were consistent with critical theory.

The conceptual framework, for example, was designed to engage the transaction between oppressive beliefs and engagement with daily activities, to counter the effects of prisonization, and to engage residents in critical dialogue about the impact of the prison environment on daily living in the community. Furthermore, it was designed to honor and give authority to the everyday experiences of the residents related to work, education, finances, social relationships, or leisure. Similarly, the initial life-skills education modules were designed to engage residents in critical dialogue about their experiences with each topic. The modules did not presume to be authoritative in how each living skill "should" be constructed in postprison life; rather the modules were each 2 weeks in length in order to ground the topics in residents' actual experiences during the week. Those actual experiences were then the basis for dialogue in Week 2 of the module. Further, in an attempt to equalize power dynamics, the modules were designed to be cofacilitated by a volunteer and a resident of the program. Therefore, several elements of this rather messy beginning seemed consistent with the beliefs of a critical evaluator.

Yet, looking back on the planning process through the belief that being self-critical can illuminate how practices maintain oppressive conditions, I have to question whose knowledge and what knowledge was dominant in this initial stage and what conditions were sustained as a result. First, my evidence-based, academic knowledge clearly carried the process. What was missed, who was missed, by my desire to have a "sound" conceptual framework in place first? What assumptions drove my need to have a process in place that was grounded in research and theory? Second, although starting with the program committee felt pragmatically necessary in order to launch initial life-skills learning modules in a short time frame, only the voices and knowledge of program planners and scholars were considered in this early phase of the project. As a result, the selection of the initial educational topics did not question the taken-for-granted authority assumed by people who had never been incarcerated about what was needed or desired by those who had; nor did the initial planning go so far as it could have to question oppressive assumptions about "life-skills training," and the motivation and capacity of residents. Instead, part of the process sustained current practice in transition programs. That is, much of the prisoner reentry programming "usually begins by forming a task force comprised of corrections professionals, academics, and state agencies. Some . . . may include ex-convicts, victims, and business and religious leaders" (Petersilia, 2004, p. 7). But few programs actually include former offenders, who use the reentry services, in the design and evaluation of a program (Petersilia, 2001; Seiter & Kadela, 2003). Prisoner reentry programs, by enforcing a programmatic agenda predetermined by external authorities, may inadvertently replicate prison dynamics, reinforcing passive behaviors, diminished skills, deference to authority, and silence on issues of importance. Therefore, reflecting on this initial phase of program evaluation and development, I would admit that, on balance, it likely served to maintain oppressive conditions for individuals in transition to the community.

"Take Two!": Subsequent (Corrective) Evaluation Process

The absence of former prisoners' voices in evaluating and designing reentry programs is significant. Therefore, after meeting the initial programming needs by launching a few new life-skills modules, I went back to the drawing board. To be more confident that the life-skills modules were addressing real needs, I needed a more complete and in-depth formative evaluation. The graduate students and I designed a process that included the residents' voices and perceptions, as well as the voices and perceptions of other stakeholders. The evaluation literature, particularly democratic approaches to program evaluation and design, was selected to guide the revised process. Democratic approaches to program evaluation begin with the premises that (a) decision making is a shared process among all parties who have an interest in a particular program or issue; and (b) the process of program evaluation has the potential to mirror and teach deliberative dialogue among diverse community citizens (see, for example, MacNeil, 2000, 2002). This participatory approach was selected intentionally, to offer residents an experience of community engagement that could counter the prison experience. That is, the evaluation team hoped that participating in the research process could provide an experience in self-efficacy, internal authority, personal causation, and deliberation with others who may hold different views. Participants included current residents in the program, their significant others, prior residents of the transition program, program staff, community volunteers, board members, and the executive director.

The Stakeholder Interviews

Group interviews were conducted to determine the perceptions of each stakeholder group about what constitutes a successful transition from prison. Interviews were conducted initially with homogeneous stakeholder groups. We planned to then follow up with discussion in heterogeneous groups about the areas of agreement and disagreement about the elements of successful transitions. This process was believed to mirror democratic community deliberation (MacNeil, 2000, 2002). Thus, through stakeholder interviews, we sought to create opportunities for residents to engage in deliberative dialogue, exercise self-efficacy, and codetermine with other stakeholders their needs for successful transition.

Problematic metaphor. A metaphor-based interview was used to explore stakeholder perceptions. The use of metaphor can aid evaluators in accessing the unspoken needs and hidden cultures within programs (Grembowski, 2001; Kaminsky, 2000; Patton, 2002; Ross, 1985). Careful to select a metaphor that conveyed "transition," a peer-review research group was convened to assess and select a metaphor, and crossing a rushing stream on a series of rocks served as the metaphor. A visual depiction of the interview was created showing an image of prison on one side, an image of a budding tree on the opposite side, representing the participants' desired futures, and a photograph of a rushing stream with stepping stones in between the images of prison and the budding tree. Each participant received the visual depiction as a worksheet for the interview. Graduate student interviewers introduced the interview to each stakeholder group as follows:

> We will utilize a picture of a rushing stream to guide our conversation today. On one side of the stream is prison. On the other side of the stream is "where you would like to be [where you would like to see residents] 5 years from now." In between prison and where you would like to be in 5 years is the stream. The stream represents the time in this program. There are 5 stepping stones for getting from one side of the stream to the other. Again, the stepping stones represent the time of transition spent here in the program. [Evaluator presents the picture and briefly describes the elements above.]

Stakeholders were first directed to the right side of the picture, the image of a budding tree, and asked to consider what they hoped life would look like 5 years from now. Residents described their hopes for themselves 5 years out; other stakeholders described their hopes for the residents 5 years out. Stakeholders were given time to consider and write down 5 hopes on the right side of the diagram. Evaluators engaged the group in a discussion of their desired futures, after which the evaluator asked the group the following:

> Now come back in time and imagine yourself arriving here at the program. You [the residents, your family member] have/has just been released from prison and you [they, he, she] are/is getting ready to cross the stream on these 5 stepping stones. These stones represent the experiences, the skills, the supports that you believe you [they, he, she] need to successfully carry you [them, him, her] from prison to the place you'd like to be in 5 years. What are the 5 most important things that will help you [them, him, her] cross the stream? Take a minute to label each stone. [Participants are given up to 10 minutes to label the stones.]

During data collection and analysis, it became apparent that the ease with which staff, board members, and the executive director accessed and responded to the metaphor image surpassed the ease with which the residents accessed and responded to the metaphor. For example, note the specificity and richness of the response given by a member of the program committee, and the possible implications such a response could have for designing a life-skills program:

The way you cross a raging stream is first of all you don't try it by yourself. And secondly you ideally want three or more people. One guy steps in and gets a firm plant and then the next guy steps in and locks arms and he gets a firm plant. Then this guy rolls over the next two and you just get rolling across. But you got two people who are stationary and not moving their feet . . . keeping that held firm and then you can move across . . . it's a great image for this situation. That's the kind of thing that you need here.

The response given by this program committee member was spontaneous. It was given immediately, without any further clarification from the interviewer. The response led to a discussion about the nature of support needed during transition.

By contrast, after the interviewers introduced the metaphor of crossing the stream to the women residents, the following dialogue ensued. Connecting with the metaphor seemed much more laborious for this stakeholder group. And responses to the metaphor like the one below led potentially back to programming that does not go beyond meeting residents' instrumental needs. In the following dialogue, the group just completed a discussion of what they desired for themselves 5 years into the future. The graduate students conducting the interview began to guide the conversation to the next part of the interview:

Evaluator 1: At this point, let's go back to the transition part of the drawing. Imagine you have just been released from prison. For some of you that may be the case right now, and for some of you, you might be a little further in your journey towards a new life you are creating. And there are stepping stones that get you across [points to the image of the stream]. Stepping stones could be skills that you have, support systems that you know of, experiences that you have or need that are going to help you reach this future life [points to the budding tree on the right side of the image]. I'd like for you to go ahead and label what those stepping stones might be . . . in helping you transition into your future life.

Participant 4: I don't understand.

Evaluator 1: The stepping stones are the things that can get you from prison to the future life that you want to create [points to the drawing]. And so what kind of skills, or what kinds of support do you need to make that future life happen? Try to think of 5 things. There could be more and that's fine too.

Participant 3: I've inhaled too much paint today. I can't sit still. . . .

[residents write for 4 minutes]

Participant 4: What are they again?

Evaluator 1: The stepping stones? They could be anything that you have, or are going to need, to help you make this transition into the future life you just described [points to drawing].

Evaluator 2: [pointing to the image] So right now you are here. You are in this program as a transition between prison [points to image] and where you want to be in the future. We want to know what you think will make it possible for you to get through this [points to stream].

[Participant 1 mumbles to the house dog]

[Participant 2 leaves the room]

Participant 1: [to the dog] I just gave you a bath last week.

Evaluator: We'll give S a few more minutes to get back.

[Participant 2 returns . . . says she just "gets like that, but now she feels better"]

Evaluator: [Draws stepping stones on a flip chart.] Okay. I drew some circles up here representing the stepping stones . . . let's try one at a time sharing with the group your number one idea—what you consider most important. Describe what came to mind when you imagined the stepping stones that might carry you to that place where life in the community is going well.

[long pause]

Participant 3: Get my license.

[Evaluator writes on the flip chart next to one of the stones she's drawn, "Get License." The group then engages in a long discussion explaining to Participant 3 how to get her license.]

It was not the case that the women's education level inhibited their participation in a discussion about transition. Several had taken, or were enrolled in, or were planning to enroll in, community college courses.

The discussion with the men also felt labored as they tried to connect with the metaphor. Like the above dialogue, the men just finished describing the elements they desire in their lives 5 years into the future. The interviewer began to direct the conversation to the next part of the interview:

Evaluator: So now imagine you are right here [points to image of the stream] . . . .Imagine that you are trying to get across to this future life we have just talked about. And if you could, please take a minute to label the five most important things that you think are going to help you create that life. It could be skills, people, experiences you bring with you or you think you'll need . . . anything you think will be most important that are going to help carry you.

Participant 1: What tools do we need? Kinda like. . . .

Evaluator: You can think of them as tools, sure.

Participant 1: Well, it's not like really tools.

Evaluator: If it's not like stepping stones in a stream, then you can use another image that might help create that. These are the things that are gonna get you

what you talked about over on this other side [points to image], the future
life you imagine. What do you need to do? What skills do you need? What
resources? What supports? Be creative.

Participant 1: Do you have an example sheet?

[long discussion about haircuts ensued]

Looking Back on Phase II: Being Self-Critical Can Illuminate How Practices Maintain Oppressive Conditions

Although Phase II was meant to be corrective of the shortcomings of Phase I,
implementing it still proved to hold elements that were both consistent and
inconsistent with the beliefs of a critical evaluator. On the consistent
side, issues of power and authority were carefully considered and strate-
gized. For example, resident groups were intentionally larger than staff
groups to allow for more voices from that stakeholder group. Graduate students, who were both part of the evaluation team and facilitators for the life-
skills modules, conducted the interviews because they had trusting
relationships with the residents and did not represent an external authority
or institution. Residents actually saw the graduate students as being more
like themselves—facing a tough system, trying to make it, better themselves,
meet goals. Like the early modules, the entire tone of the interview was
designed to convey and respect the actual experiences, efficacy, and personal
agency of the residents. Finally, the interview was designed to engage multiple modes of participating, for example, auditory, visual, imaginative, cognitive, and kinesthetic modes.

   Yet, looking back on the interviews in Phase II through the belief that
being self-critical can illuminate how practices maintain oppressive conditions, I have to question the selection and use of the metaphor. First, I used
the expertise of researchers, many of whom were critical theorists, to
explore relevant metaphors. I failed to explore with participants in the program what a transition from prison feels like and thus failed to derive the
metaphor from their experience. Second, it seems rather obvious, and somewhat embarrassing looking back now, but we also failed to consider the
socioeconomic issues embedded in the metaphor of crossing a rushing
stream. Who, generally, experiences crossing a rushing stream? Probably
people like me, who have had opportunities for being in wilderness or
national park areas, which usually involves access to transportation and
money for travel and for gear that works well in outdoor environments. By
contrast, many residents in the program came from backgrounds of poverty
and many from poor, urban environments. Therefore, because the metaphor
was problematic, residents, their significant others, and former residents
may have been deprived of their potential descriptive power for what constitutes a successful transition from prison. Consequently, rather than
empowering the ones who use the life-skills program to have a major say in

what the program became, the metaphor may have diminished their voices and lessened their say. This is particularly troublesome in that the interview process, designed to counter the dynamics of prisonization, may have inadvertently reinforced them by choosing a metaphor to which some residents had only veiled access.

Drawing on the work by Lakoff and Johnson (2003), Kaminsky (2000) stated that "metaphors are used consciously, but are in use unconsciously" (p. 70). It is common practice for evaluators to attend to the metaphors that are in use unconsciously by stakeholders. But in this case, one metaphor selected as an evaluation tool was simultaneously used consciously and was in use unconsciously. In use unconsciously, metaphors frame problems and circumstances in particular ways. Unconsciously, a rushing stream frames transition to the community as a very dangerous, treacherous, precarious situation. As indicated by recidivism rates, navigating the transition can indeed be treacherous for some. But missing from the metaphor is the celebration of completing one's restitution, returning to one's community, reclaiming one's own life, and the possibility of a new start. Framing the transition with a metaphor of danger perhaps restricted the potential responses to what is needed during transition. Therefore, without careful critical evaluation of metaphors within the life context of program stakeholders, metaphors can also marginalize stakeholder groups and prevent full participation in the program evaluation process.

In sum, the belief that being self-critical can illuminate how practices maintain oppressive conditions was a useful guide for reflecting on an evaluation with a transition program for individuals returning to the community from prison. Both the weak and strong elements of the process contained features that were consistent and inconsistent with being a critical evaluator. It is humbling to consider that a process that on the whole sought to counter oppressive dynamics, instead, in unexpected ways, actually maintained oppressive conditions of people making their way to, ironically, community citizenship. Like the folks transitioning to the community, who keep falling forward into self-determined routines and activities, I keep falling forward into the beliefs and assumptions Freeman and Vasconcelos (this issue) set before us, stumbling as I go on the internalized needs, interests, and knowledge from my own life context.

References

Austin, J., Irwin, J., & Hardyman, P. (2002, January). Exploring the needs and risks of the returning prisoner population. In *Proceedings from the National Policy Conference: From Prison to Home: The Effect of Incarceration and Re-Entry on Children, Families, and Communities* (pp. 54–76). Washington, DC: The Urban Institute.

Christiansen, C. H. (1999). The 1999 Eleanor Clarke Slagle Lecture—Defining lives: Occupation as identity: An essay on competence, coherence, and the creation of meaning. *American Journal of Occupational Therapy, 53*(6), 547–558.

Cranton, P. (1994). Self-directed and transformative instructional development. *Journal of Higher Education, 65*(6), 726–744.

Cranton, P. (2002). Teaching for transformation. In J. M. Ross-Gordon (Ed.), *Contemporary viewpoints on teaching adults effectively. New Directions for Adult and Continuing Education, 93,* 63–71.

Dirkx, J. M. (2001). The power of feelings: Emotion, imagination, and the construction of meaning in adult learning. In S. B. Merriam (Ed.), *The new update on adult learning theory. New Directions for Adult and Continuing Education, 89,* 63–72.

Dirkx, J., & Prenger, S. (1997). *Planning and implementing instruction for adults: A theme-based approach.* San Francisco: Jossey-Bass.

Grembowski, D. (2001). *The practice of health program evaluation.* Thousand Oaks, CA: Sage.

Haney, C. (2002, January). The psychological impact of incarceration: Implications for post-prison adjustment. In *Proceedings from the National Policy Conference: From Prison to Home: The Effect of Incarceration and Re-Entry on Children, Families, and Communities* (pp. 1–19). Washington, DC: The Urban Institute.

Horowitz, B., & Chang, P. F. (2004). Promoting well-being and engagement in life through occupational therapy lifestyle redesign: A pilot study with adult day programs. *Topics in Geriatric Rehabilitation, 20*(1), 46–58.

Jackson, J., Carlson, M., Mandel, D., Zemke, R., & Clark, F. (1998). Occupation in lifestyle redesign: The well-elderly occupational therapy program. *American Journal of Occupational Therapy, 52*(5), 326–336.

Kaminsky, A. (2000). Beyond the literal: Metaphors and why they matter. In R. Hopson (Ed.), *How and why language matters in evaluation. New Directions for Evaluation, 86,* 69–80).

Kegan, R. (2000). What "form" transforms? A constructive–developmental approach to transformative learning. In J. Mezirow (Ed.), *Learning as transformation: Critical perspectives on a theory in progress* (pp. 35–70). San Francisco: Jossey-Bass.

Kielhofner, G. (2002). *A model of human occupation: Theory and practice.* Baltimore: Lippincott, Williams & Wilkins.

Lakoff, G., & Johnson, M. (2003). *Metaphors we live by.* Chicago: University of Chicago Press.

Lawton, M. P. (1982). Competence, environmental press, and the adaptation of old people. In M. P. Lawton, P. G. Windley, & T. O. Byers (Eds.), *Aging and the environment: Theoretical approaches* (pp. 33–59). New York: Springer.

Lipschutz, E. G. (2002). Perceived experiences of well senior women engaged in occupational lifestyle redesign. *Occupational Therapy Journal of Research, 22,* 97S–98S.

MacNeil, C. (2000). Surfacing the realpolitik: Democratic evaluation in an antidemocratic climate. In K. Ryan & L. DeStefano (Eds.), *Evaluation as democratic process: Promoting deliberation, dialogue, and inclusion. New Directions for Evaluation, 85,* 51–62.

MacNeil, C. (2002). Evaluator as steward of citizen deliberation. *American Journal of Evaluation, 23*(1), 45–54.

McAdams, D. P. (1997). *The stories we live by: Personal myths and the making of the self.* New York: Guilford Press.

Mezirow, J. (Ed.). (2000). *Learning as transformation: Critical perspectives on a theory in progress.* San Francisco: Jossey-Bass.

Patton, M. Q. (2002). *Qualitative research and evaluation methods* (3rd ed.). Thousand Oaks, CA: Sage.

Petersilia, J. (2001). Prisoner reentry: Public safety and reintegration challenges. *Prison Journal, 81*(3), 360–375.

Petersilia, J. (2004). What works in prisoner reentry? Reviewing and questioning the evidence. *Federal Probation, 68*(2), 4–8.

Ross, J. A. (1985). Program evaluation as problem solving. *Evaluation Review, 9*(6), 659–679.

Seiter, R. P., & Kadela, K. R. (2003). Prisoner reentry: What works, what does not, and what is promising. *Crime & Delinquency, 49*(3), 360–388.

Travis, J., Solomon, A., & Waul, M. (2001). *From prison to home: The dimensions and consequences of prisoner re-entry.* Washington, DC: The Urban Institute.

BARBARA HOOPER is assistant professor in occupational therapy and director of the Center for Occupational Therapy Education at Colorado State University; her research and professional development initiatives focus on transformative learning, particularly how assumptions relate to actions in teaching and learning contexts.

NEW DIRECTIONS FOR EVALUATION • DOI: 10.1002/ev

3

Critical Development? Using a Critical Theory Lens to Examine the Current Role of Evaluation in the Youth-Development Field

Sarah Zeller-Berkman

Abstract

A critical theory lens is used to explore the role of evaluation in youth development, a field aimed at recognizing youth as assets. A theory of change in the field is questioned for its emphasis on individual youth outcomes as programmatic outcome measures. A review of 209 evaluations of 131 programs in the Harvard Family Research Project's Out-of-School Time Program Research and Evaluation Database reveals an overemphasis on individual gains related to academic achievement or youth development and a lack of attention to community- or systems-level outcomes. The author posits that a critical approach would press evaluators to be intentional about what they measure and how in order to challenge the status quo for young people. © Wiley Periodicals, Inc., and the American Evaluation Association.

The increase in funding for youth development under former President Bush to $3.6 billion in annual federal funding (Padgette, 2003) is in part because of heavy investment in research and evaluation (Little, Wimer, & Weiss, 2008). The youth-development field in the United States is set to receive unprecedented amounts of funding from the current

New Directions for Evaluation, no. 127, Fall 2010 © Wiley Periodicals, Inc., and the American Evaluation Association. Published online in Wiley Online Library (wileyonlinelibrary.com) • DOI: 10.1002/ev.337

U.S. government administration. Evaluations have demonstrated that after-school programs can remediate poor academic performance, prevent violence and drug use, improve health and wellness, and increase the self-esteem of young people (Little et al., 2008). However, even with increased funding and positive research findings, young people are still over-incarcerated, hypervillanized, and lack a say on many issues that affect their lives. I argue here that a flawed theory of change for the field and the consistent focus of youth-program evaluations on individual rather than communal changes contribute to maintaining the low power status for young people in the United States.

Critical social theorists critique processes and structures that maintain the status quo, they are "critical of what they see as pervasive inequalities and injustices in everyday social relationships and arrangements" (Freeman & Vasconcelos, this issue). A critical social theory reveals underlying assumptions, and concerns itself with forms of authority and injustice by assessing how things are in order to transform them into what they ought to be. This chapter has three major goals: (a) to conduct a critical analysis of youth-development evaluations to reveal how the field perpetuates the status quo for young people in the United States, (b) to present a vision of what "ought to be" by exploring alternative evaluation designs that challenge traditional power dynamics between adults and young people, and (c) to imagine how evaluation in the youth-development field could help support a critical agenda.

The Low Power Status of Young People in the United States

The concept of ageism is not new, although the assumption that young people are in a low power position and therefore a low power group in the United States may not be a commonly held view. A review of the literature related to young people in the United States reveals a grim and somewhat surprising picture. The United States affords its young people fewer rights in relation to adults than any other country (Males, 2006). There are 14.1 million persons under the age of 18 in poverty (U.S. Census Bureau, 2008) and they are two to three times more likely to live in poverty than middle-aged adults (Males, 2006). Amnesty International (2004) reports that the United States has conducted half the world's executions of persons for crimes committed as youth since 1990. Additionally, the United States is the only self-governed nation in the world that has failed to ratify the United Nations Convention on the Rights of the Child that would guarantee benefits such as adequate nutrition, housing, recreation, and medical services.

In addition to these very tangible inequities experienced by young people, the adult public at large also perceives them quite negatively. For example, 57% of adults believe that today's children and teens will make America a worse place or will make little difference in the future (Camino & Zeldin, 2006). Similarly, 66% of adults believe the percentage of teens who committed violent crimes had increased in recent years, when in reality it had declined (Camino & Zeldin, 2006). Public Agenda polling done in 1997 (Farkas, Johnson, Duffett, & Bers, 1997) found that adults of all backgrounds agree that youth today are "undisciplined, disrespectful, and unfriendly." Two-thirds of Americans (67%) immediately reached for negative adjectives, such as *rude*, *irresponsible*, and *wild*, whereas only 12% used positive terms, such as *smart* or *helpful*.

Negative representations, coupled with youth isolation from day-to-day supportive contact with adults and intergenerational community life outside of school, have made it easy to convince adults that young people are unable to contribute to community in positive ways (Kirshner, 2006; Males, 2006; Zeldin, Larson, Camino, & O'Conner, 2005). Zeldin and Topitzes (2002) found that less than 25% of urban adults had a great deal of confidence that adolescents could represent their community in front of city council or serve as a voting member of a community organization. The media, child-related institutions and policies, and our age-segregated society weave together to form a net around young people that provides little room to alter these very prescribed and limited roles (Zeldin, Camino, & Calvert, 2003). That net is further constricted by adult disinterest in creating the conditions for youth empowerment. A national study conducted by Benson, Scales, Leffert, and Roehlkepartain (2001) found that when adults were asked to rate the relative importance of 19 actions that communities could take on behalf of young people, the two actions reflective of youth engagement received the lowest ratings. These actions were "seek young people's opinions when making decisions that affect them" and "give young people lots of opportunities to make their communities better places." In a study conducted by Benson (1998) of 460 communities, only 35% of youth reported that their community values youth and youth are given useful roles. It is no wonder then that Males (1996) asserts that young people remain one of the few groups that society is systematically permitted to exclude.

Although adults are generally unwilling to create the conditions under which youth can take action on their own behalf, youth are simultaneously framed as in need of protection by adults. Many youth are roped into child protection agencies that have failed children egregiously, for "their own good" (Lowry, 2004). The desire to create policy to protect young people resonates for both conservatives and progressives alike (Lakoff, 2004).

The statistics are disturbingly clear; youth on the whole have little power and are characterized in a plethora of negative social representations. It is important to point out that oppression plays out differently for privileged, white, straight and/or male youth (Ginwright & James, 2002). This article interrogates evaluation's role in maintaining the low power status of young people in the United States by placing the youth-development field and evaluation under a critical gaze, magnifying the ways in which a field aimed at shifting the status quo for young people inadvertently maintains it.

New Directions for Evaluation • DOI: 10.1002/ev

Evaluation of Youth Development

Perpetuating Status Quo

Postmodern critical theorists traced the way knowledge and power is produced in discursive formations, thereby unmasking their effects on the construction of multiple subjects in society (Leonard, 1990). Here, I will critique the discursive formations of a theory-of-change model that articulates the relationship between community and young people for the youth-development field. The fact that this theory of change may be fundamentally flawed has tremendous implications, as it is used for strategic planning, ongoing decision making, and, most importantly for this article, evaluation (Gambone, 2006). As theory-of-change models are often used to guide evaluation, one may assume that the critique leveled would be confirmed by looking at actual evaluations in the field.

The theory of change used for this analysis needed to meet two standards: (a) summarize theoretical frameworks across major thinkers and/or institutions in the youth-development field, and (b) use data from a variety of sources. Gambone (2006) analyzed 25 theoretical frameworks, community initiatives, and projects for a common vision of outcomes and process to create a theory of change about youth development and communities (see Figure 3.1).

The long-term outcomes for youth identified across youth-development models are: (a) economic self-sufficiency, such as adequate education, living-wage jobs, and discretionary resources; (b) healthy family and social relationships, such as physical and mental health, good caregivers/parents, and dependable family and friendship networks; and (c) community involvement as taxpayers, law-abiding citizens, voters, and members of churches and other organizations.

In order to achieve these outcomes, Gambone (2006) indicates that youth-development interventions rally individuals, institutions, systems, and organizations to contribute to community outcomes that support youth development. These community outcomes then contribute to individual youth support and opportunities for development, such as supportive relationships with adults and peers; challenging and interesting learning experiences; and meaningful opportunities for involvement, membership, and safety. The individual youth supports and opportunities for development lead to positive youth psychological processes and increased competencies that purportedly produce the outcomes for youth.

What is striking in this theory of change for the field is that all arrows point to clear and measurable outcomes for youth. The support of individuals (assumed in this model to be adults), institutions, systems, and organizations are all focused on developing young people into competent and productive adults. There is a unidirectional flow of support for development that starts from adults and ends up as development outcomes for youth.

NEW DIRECTIONS FOR EVALUATION • DOI: 10.1002/ev

Figure 3.1. A Model of the Relationship Between Youth Development and Adult Communities

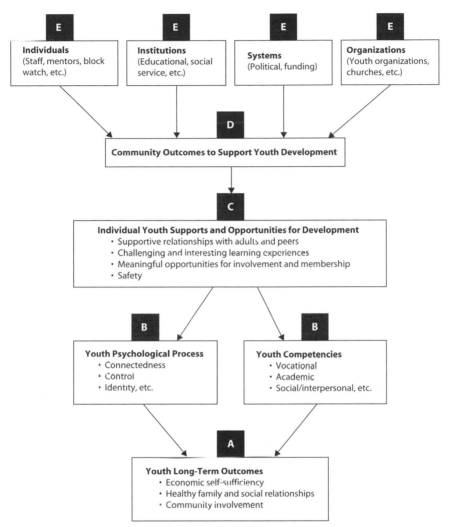

The depositing of development into young people who act as receptacles as opposed to actors who shoot back arrows of development toward adults, institutions, systems, and society is reminiscent of what critical theorist Paulo Freire (1970) refers to as the *banking concept* in education. Development, like education, becomes an act of depositing, in which young people are the repositories and the adults are the depositors. This thinking maintains the view that young people have nothing to offer that would simultaneously contribute to the development of adults, institutions, systems, and organizations. Freire (1970) viewed oppressed people as potential actors and sources of knowledge and active contributors to their own liberation. This model does not portray young people as assets to society, but only in need of society's attention, protection, guidance, and development. Although it is valuable to meet young people's needs, by not recognizing that young people are able to contribute to their own development and that of others, including adults, the model maintains traditional representations of youth. The fact that the theory of change for the field may be fundamentally flawed has tremendous implications, because these models often guide decisions and evaluations of programs that affect youth.

As theory-of-change models are often used to guide evaluation, it becomes important to understand what kinds of outcomes are targeted by evaluations, and in what way they contribute to or alter the prevalent focus on individual development. In order to portray an overview of evaluation work in the field of out-of-school time (OST) to test the claim that most youth-development evaluations serve to maintain the status quo for young people, I analyzed one of the only comprehensive databases in the OST field, the Harvard Family Research Project's (HFRP) Out-of-School Time Program Research and Evaluation Database. This database contains over 209 evaluations of both large and small out-of-school time programs and initiatives. HFRP solicited evaluations and studies from multiple sources, including scanning the OST field; OST, research, and evaluation listservs; researchers and evaluators; and people who have contacted them about their OST work.

The evaluation profiles in this database are searchable on key criteria in each of these broad categories. I utilized this search mechanism to refine my scan of the profiles to specific program, research, and evaluation characteristics, and findings. I conducted three types of scans. In the first scan I searched for community or systemic outcomes for evaluations of middle school and high school programs. That search revealed no matches. For the second search I looked for all evaluations that had community outcomes and found 4 out of 209 evaluations that measured outcomes at that level. The last search, for systemic outcomes, revealed two evaluations and a literacy project. Out of 209 unreplicated evaluation designs, only a handful measured community- or systems-level outcomes, while the majority measured individual gains related to academic achievement and youth-development outcomes. The small number of hits on evaluations that reported community-level outcomes reflect the field's focus on the individual as the object of development and change instead of looking for multiple levels of impact that may address root causes of inequity. Transforming evaluation questions on outcomes that are not just located in youth may move the youth-development field toward social justice for young people, adults, and communities, altering power relations on many levels. Thinking about what a critical approach would bring to evaluation requires that we interrogate what evaluative processes can examine root causes as well as alter traditional power dynamics.

NEW DIRECTIONS FOR EVALUATION • DOI: 10.1002/ev

Moving Toward Greater Alignment: What Ought to Be

Freeman and Vasconcelos (this issue) posit that critical theory offers a new vision for evaluation that is "participatory, pedagogical, and action oriented." One such evaluation design that meets those criteria and moves evaluation in the field of youth development toward more alignment between theory and practice is youth participatory evaluation (YPE). In 2003, *New Directions for Evaluation* published a groundbreaking issue on youth participatory evaluation. With the use of empowering practices developed in action research and participatory evaluation, Sabo's (2003) work fostered a shift in the youth-development field toward an asset model where youth are seen as problem solvers. This approach counteracts the prevailing deficit model in which youth are seen as problems to be solved. Like other researchers (Camino, 1992; Camino & Zeldin, 1999; Checkoway & Finn, 1992; Pittman & Wright, 1991), Sabo (2003) argued that "the participation of young people in research and evaluation. . . could not only generate knowledge about— but also provide opportunities for—the development of young participants and the empowerment of their communities" (p. 5).

These gains are not purely theoretical. For example, the youth-led research, evaluation, and planning (youth REP) approach developed by Youth in Focus (2002) offers youth meaningful leadership opportunities and addresses critical issues of power and social inequality (London, Zimmerman, & Erbstein, 2003). It does so by offering training and coaching in research and evaluation on multiple levels: youth participants, on-site project facilitators, and executive leadership. The Youth REP process also moves from training to actions by supporting sites to plan for the implementation of the youth produced recommendations. Youth in Focus views youth-led evaluation as an ongoing process of critical inquiry and improvement (London et al., 2003). Documented gains for young people include, for example, the development of strong research, analytical and writing skills, and civic engagement. Other benefits included improvements in organizational program campaigns, service effectiveness, and new understandings of community issues. Lastly, communities gained increased capacity to support intergenerational partnerships and social capital through youth leaders and proactive and creative approaches to community building (London et al., 2003).

The gains for young people, adults, programs, communities, and the field of evaluation that are derived from involving young people in evaluation work have been well documented (Lau, Netherland, & Haywood, 2003; London, 2002; London et al., 2003; Sabo, 2003; Wheeler, 2000). Other designs, like democratic evaluation, deliberative democratic evaluation, and communicative evaluation, may have similar transformative potential. Regardless of the particular design, evaluators must consider the impact of their process and results for ways that it stymies or promotes social transformation.

NEW DIRECTIONS FOR EVALUATION • DOI: 10.1002/ev

Supporting a Critical Agenda

How can evaluation support and develop a critical agenda that would strive to change some of the oppressive conditions and social representations of young people in the United States today? One possible solution is using a process, like youth participatory evaluation, that reflects the belief that young people are in fact assets and have valuable knowledge that would contribute to improving programs and services of the organization. By involving young people and heeding their research we are challenging traditional conceptions of the role of young people and the notion of "expertise."

By focusing our evaluative eyes on more than just young people's development we can highlight or problematize the adult-level changes, program-level changes, and community-level changes that result from intentional youth-development programs. Like other researchers in the field (Pittman, Martin, & Williams, 2007), I posit that the outcomes so desired for young people are not attainable when the focus is only on their individual development. There are social conditions and institutions that also need to change in order for young people to fight back against the forces that constrict their growth. Moving in this direction requires transforming both the theory of change for the youth-development field to one that posits developmental outcomes not only for youth, but for adults, programs, communities, and institutions. Arrows in a theory of change would be bidirectional and reflect how youth are not just objects to be developed, but change agents. Evaluators would be pushed to develop more complex measures to capture change at multiple levels and not solely survey young people at the end of their program year to measure how much their self-confidence has improved or how many negative behaviors they are or are not engaging in (for strong examples of community or advocacy evaluation, see Coffman, 2007, and Louie & Guthrie, 2007).

Evaluators may have to work with young people to make sure the questions they ask do not reinforce negative conceptions of young people and check that the methods used be interrogated for the ways in which they are participatory or pedagogical. A critical approach would challenge evaluators to be intentional of both what they do and how they do evaluative work.

Conclusion

The current use of evaluation in the field of youth development serves to maintain the status quo for young people. Critical theory offers a lens through which one can interrogate the misalignment between the field's theory of how change happens for young people and the foundations of a field that posits that young people are capable of contributing to the development of themselves, adults, programs, communities, and society as a whole. Critical evaluation not only pushes one to consider the theoretical misalignment of theory and practice, but moves us to take action. In a time when trends in evaluation are moving farther from youth participation and toward experimental designs focused on individual-level outcomes, evaluators are encouraged to take a critical stance and actively push back against reinforcing the status quo for the participants in the programs they evaluate.

References

Amnesty International. (2004). *Execution of child offenders since 1990.* Retrieved August 22, 2006, from http://web.amnesty.org/pages/deathpenalty-children-stats-eng

Benson, P. L. (1998). *Mobilizing communities to promote developmental assets: A promising strategy for the prevention of high risk behaviors.* Minneapolis, MN: Search Institute.

Benson, P. L., Scales, P. C., Leffert, N., & Roehlkepartain, E. C. (2001). *A fragile foundation: The state of developmental assets among American youth.* Minneapolis, MN: Search Institute.

Camino, L. (1992). *What differences do racial, ethnic, and cultural differences make in youth development programs?* Washington, DC: Carnegie Council on Adolescent Development.

Camino, L., & Zeldin, S. (1999). Youth leadership: Linking research and program theory to exemplary practice. *New Designs for Youth Development, 15,* 10–15.

Camino, L., & Zeldin, S. (2006). Adult roles in youth activism. In L. R. Sherrod (Ed.), *Youth activism: An international encyclopedia* (Vol. 1, pp. 34–38). Westport, CT: Greenwood.

Checkoway, B., & Finn, J. (1992). *Young people as community builders.* Ann Arbor: School of Social Work, University of Michigan.

Coffman, J. (2007). What's different about evaluation advocacy and policy change? *The Evaluation Exchange, 12*(1). Retrieved June 1, 2009, from http://www.gse.harvard.edu/hfrp/eval/

Farkas, S., Johnson, J., Duffett, A., & Bers, A. (1997). *Kids these days: What Americans really think about the next generation?* New York: Public Agenda.

Freire, P. (1970). *Pedagogy of the oppressed.* New York: Continuum.

Gambone, M. A. (2006). Community action and youth development: What can be done and how can we measure progress? In K. Fulbright-Anderson & P. Auspos (Eds.), *Community change: Theories, practice, and evidence* (pp. 269–321). Aspen Institute Roundtable on Community Change. Washington, DC: Aspen Institute.

Ginwright, S., & James, T. (2002). From assets to agents of change: Social justice, organizing, and youth development. In B. Kirshner, J. L. O'Donoghue, & M. McLaughlin (Eds.), *Youth participation: Improving institutions and communities. New Directions for Youth Development, 96,* 27–46.

Kirshner, B. (2006). Apprenticeship learning and youth activism. In S. Ginwright, P. Noguera, & J. Cammarota (Eds.), *Beyond resistance! Youth activism and community change* (pp. 37–57). New York: Routledge.

Lakoff, G. (2004). *Don't think of an elephant! Know your values and frame the debate: The essential guide for progressives.* White River Junction, VT: Chelsea Green.

Lau, G., Netherland, N. H., & Haywood, M. L. (2003). Youth-led research and evaluation: Tools for youth, organizational, and community development. In K. Sabo (Ed.), *Youth participatory evaluation: A field in the making. New Directions for Evaluation, 98,* 47–59.

Leonard, S. T. (1990). *Critical theory in political practice.* Princeton, NJ: Princeton University Press.

Little, P., Wimer, C., & Weiss, H. B. (2008). After school programs in the 21st century: Their potential and what it takes to achieve it. *Issues and opportunities in out-of-school time evaluation* (Vol. 10). Cambridge, MA: Harvard Family Research Project.

London, J. (2002, June). *Youth involvement in community research and evaluation: Mapping the field.* Paper presented at the Wingspread Symposium on Youth Involvement in Community Research and Evaluation, Racine, WI. Retrieved June 23, 2010, from http://www.ssw.umich.edu/youthandcommunity/pubs/London_YouthResEval.pdf

London, J., Zimmerman, K., & Erbstein, N. (2003). Youth-led research, evaluation and planning as youth, organizational and community development. In K. Sabo (Ed.), *Youth participatory evaluation: A field in the making. New Directions for Evaluation, 98,* 33–45.

Louie, J., & Guthrie, K. (2007). Strategies for assessing policy change efforts: A prospective approach. *The Evaluation Exchange, 12*(1). Retrieved June 1, 2009, from http://www.gse.harvard.edu/hfrp/eval/

Lowry, M. R. (2004). Putting teeth into ASFA: The need for statutory minimum standards. *Children and Youth Services Review, 26*(11), 1021–1031.

Males, M. (1996). *The scapegoat generation: America's war on adolescents.* Monroe, ME: Common Courage Press.

Males, M. (2006). Youth policy and institutional change. In S. Ginwright, P. Noguera, & J. Cammarota (Eds.), *Beyond resistance! Youth activism and community change* (pp. 301–318). New York: Routledge.

Padgette, H. C. (2003). *Finding funding: A guide to federal sources for out-of-school time and community school initiatives, revised and updated.* Washington DC: The Finance Project. Retrieved from http://76.12.61.196/publications/FundingGuide2003.pdf

Pittman, K., Martin, S., & Williams, A. (2007). *Core principles for engaging young people in community change.* Washington, DC: The Forum for Youth Investment, Impact Strategies, Inc.

Pittman, K., & Wright, M. (1991). *Bridging the gap: A rationale for enhancing the role of community organizations in promoting youth development and community programs at the Carnegie Council on adolescent development.* Washington, DC: Center for Youth Development and Policy Research.

Sabo, K. (2003). A Vygotskian perspective on youth participatory evaluation. In K. Sabo (Ed.), *Youth participatory evaluation: A field in the making. New Directions for Evaluation, 98,* 13–24.

U.S. Census Bureau. (2008). *Income, poverty, and health insurance coverage in the United States* (P60-236, Table B-2). Retrieved from http://www.census.gov/prod/2009pubs/p60-236.pdf

Wheeler, W. (2000). Emerging organizational theory and the youth development. *Applied Developmental Science, 4*(Suppl. l), 47–54.

Youth in Focus. (2002). *Youth REP step by step: An introduction to youth-led research, evaluation and planning.* Oakland, CA: Youth in Focus.

Zeldin, S., Camino, L., & Calvert, M. (2003). Towards an understanding of youth engagement in community governance: Policy priorities and research directions. *Social Policy Report, XVII*(111).

Zeldin, S., Larson, R., Camino, L., & O'Conner, C. (2005). Intergenerational relationships and partnerships in community programs: Purpose, practice and directions for research. *Journal of Community Psychology, 33*(1), 1–10.

Zeldin, S., & Topitzes, D. (2002). Neighborhood experiences, community connection, and positive beliefs about adolescents among urban adults and youth. *Journal of Community Psychology, 30*(6), 647–669.

SARAH ZELLER-BERKMAN is a doctoral candidate at the CUNY Graduate Center and the director of the Beacons National Strategy Initiative for the Youth Development Institute in New York City. She has worked in partnership with young people on participatory action research projects and as an evaluator of youth-development initiatives.

Freeman, M., Preissle, J., & Havick, S. (2010). Moral knowledge and responsibilities in evaluation implementation: When critical theory and responsive evaluation collide. In
M. Freeman (Ed.), *Critical social theory and evaluation practice*. New Directions for Evaluation, 127, 45–57.

4

Moral Knowledge and Responsibilities in Evaluation Implementation: When Critical Theory and Responsive Evaluation Collide

Melissa Freeman, Judith Preissle, Steven Havick

Abstract

*An external evaluation documented what occurred in an inaugural summer
camp to teach high school students how to preserve religious freedom by learning about and acting on the history and current state of church–state separation
and other first amendment issues. Camp designers hoped to promote religious
diversity values and civic engagement in youth. An analytic vignette grounded
in an inductive analysis of observations, interviews, and document collection
represents the competing demands of responsive and critical approaches to evaluation. Balancing obligations to promote the social well-being of society with
responsibilities to clients and other stakeholders presents challenges that can be
met only by identifying priorities with clients in ongoing dialogue.* © Wiley
Periodicals, Inc., and the American Evaluation Association.

W hat does it mean for evaluators to be morally responsible? The
American Evaluation Association (AEA, 2004) Guiding Principles for Evaluators, developed in 1994 and ratified in 2004, suggests an ethics of responsible professional action. These include openly
disclosing the strengths and limitations of the evaluation's design and
process, respecting diverse individual needs and perspectives, and maxi-
mizing benefits and minimizing harms. The final principle, responsibility

NEW DIRECTIONS FOR EVALUATION, no. 127, Fall 2010 © Wiley Periodicals, Inc., and the American Evaluation
Association.   Published online in Wiley Online Library (wileyonlinelibrary.com) • DOI: 10.1002/ev.338

for general and public welfare, however, pushes evaluators to go beyond a responsive evaluation design to one that engages with evaluation practice more critically and reflexively. It requires that evaluators balance client and stakeholder welfare with that of the broader community (Schwandt, 2007).

We agree with Segerholm (2003), who argues that all evaluations become part of the fabric of everyday institutional and social practice and play a role in how societies function and change. Embracing a critical stance, then, means more than criticizing one's methodological approach; it means considering intended and unintended consequences of evaluation decisions. In a democratic society evaluators are responsible for identifying and challenging program and evaluation processes that disempower, oppress, exclude, misrepresent, or dismiss particular stakeholders or stakeholder views, practices, and discourses, while alternatively identifying and understanding program and evaluation processes that are inclusive, democratic, and empowering. Furthermore, a critical orientation for evaluation is necessarily self-reflexive of its own practice and how that practice serves to empower or disempower our client, those our client serves, and society. This involves the kind of reflexivity Macbeth (2001) describes as "the turning back of an inquiry or a theory or a text onto its own formative possibilities" (p. 36). Only through this kind of self-examination can we understand what we mean when we talk about our responsibility for general and public welfare. In this chapter, we examine some of the difficulties of putting this principle into practice and consider the role moral discourse might play in supporting its facilitation.

The program we evaluated, and that challenged our responsibility for the general welfare, was a camp collaboratively run by a liberal religious group and a national advocacy organization devoted to religious diversity in civic life. Combining camp activities (such as cabin council, human bingo, and field games) with academic sessions (such as lectures on the first amendment, workshops on conflict resolution and cultural diversity) and advocacy groups to develop action plans, the collaborating founders from the two groups designed a week-long program. Their goal was to provide 29 religiously and culturally diverse high school students with what the founders believed to be the necessary knowledge, skills, and values for the youth to act as leaders in their local communities against threats to religious liberty. The founders' intention was to develop a program model that they could reproduce across the United States. Joining the founders about a year after the initiative was conceived, we three evaluators participated in the planning sessions for the program in December 2005, we provided an interim report the following March, we were on site for the program in August 2006, and we submitted our evaluation report to the founders the following fall.

We used a responsive approach because our clients wanted us to document the evolving understandings and issues stakeholders had about the program, as well as provide feedback on the quality of the participants' experience (Abma, 2006; Greene & Abma, 2001). Furthermore, the founding team emphasized collaboration, dialogue, and responsiveness to each other, qualities inherent to responsive evaluation (Abma, 2006), so we built our participant observations, interviews, and focus groups into their nascent design. Our intent was to witness and elicit their value perspectives, agreements, and disagreements as they were occurring. Overall, our report was positive because the experiences the youth reported, and we observed, were positive. However, several issues arose during implementation and after the program ended that challenged us to reassess the effect our actions and inactions may have had on the collaborative democratic process the founders had aspired to, but had failed to achieve. This chapter reflects on what we witnessed happening during program implementation, the ethical issues these events raised for us, how we considered them in our report, and how we might have addressed them in light of what has occurred since dissemination of the report. Central to our argument is that dialogue should generate a critical awareness of the interrelatedness of knowledge and values so that stakeholders can develop a better understanding of the reasons for their agreements and disagreements while they are having them, not retrospectively, when reading the evaluation report (Beiner, 1983, p. 152).

The chapter is organized around a narrative vignette (Erickson, 1986; Humphreys, 2005; Polkinghorne, 1995) highlighting core programmatic issues that were dividing the founding group. The incident that the vignette dramatically reconstructs stands out because it represents the magnitude of competing issues faced by the founding group. It shows the emotional response of the group when faced with several students who did not seem at first to represent the kind of student they had expected (i.e., academically engaged), and how conceding to charismatic authority can hamper democratic decision making. In our discussion of these issues, we question whether and how we could have played a more active role in pushing for a moral discourse about "what is right to do in a given situation" (Schwandt, 2002, p. 7) among the stakeholders involved. Whether explicitly spoken or not spoken at all, how we act and interact with others, as people or evaluators, carries moral value, and in turn this moral value affects the practice and outcome of the evaluation and the program evaluated.

The Camp Devoted to Religious Diversity in Civic Life

Cast of Characters

The founding team of 20 adults was comprised of people in their 20s and 30s, some of whom worked for the camp and had training in youth programming and others of whom worked for the national organization as advocates for religious liberty, and people in their 60s and 70s, most of whom were retired civic or academic professionals recruited by Frankie, a retired public-relations professional and long-time board member of the

Figure 4.1. Program Personnel in the Program to Promote Diversity in Civic Life

national advocacy organization. Frankie was the impetus behind the program and the identified leader of the entire group. She had contacted the people at the liberal camp, located two curriculum developers to translate the group's ideas into a program, and hired the evaluation team to show evidence of success for funding purposes. Figure 4.1 depicts the groups associated with this program.

Vignette: A Program for Diversity Balks When Diversity Arrives

The vignette that follows is written in Melissa Freeman's voice to portray the events as one of us experienced them; it draws on field notes, not audiorecordings, collected during the August program, so none of the attributed quotes can be considered verbatim of what was actually said by us or any of the participants involved. They are written as quotes to retain the evocative purpose of the vignette.

> It is mid-afternoon, first full day of the week-long program. I enter the cabin where Jude and Steve have been waiting for me while I attended one of the program founders' daily debriefing sessions. "You won't believe what I have just witnessed," I tell them. "They are going to send the Black kids home!" "Are you serious?" Steve questions, "I mean, this morning, while Tim lectured, Deangelo was sitting there covering his ears with his hands and letting out loud sighs, Dominique was playing with her water bottle, and Jorell was going back and forth from being restless to feigning sleep. Certainly that is

NEW DIRECTIONS FOR EVALUATION • DOI: 10.1002/ev

behavior that needs to be corrected, but it isn't something that should get a kid sent home!" "It's true," I exclaim. "It didn't take them long to offer that as a solution. But it started with Kelli being concerned with the youths' behavior during the teaching and then somehow it developed into a recruitment issue and then this."

The first academic session had just ended that morning in the large room. The issue prompting Kelli, one of the camp's associates, to call the meeting was the different levels of engagement she had noticed among the 29 high school students during their first academic session on the history of the first amendment in the United States. The students had sat in three semicircles in chairs facing Tim and Marge, the two instructors, while adults not teaching that day sat around near the back. Three Black teens sat restless, making faces and giggling, their heads and faces partially buried under large sweatshirt hoods. Among the students were a small handful of interested participants (a Muslim, a Sikh, a Christian, two Universalist Unitarians), who responded to the bulk of the questions, while the rest of the diverse group of students sat quietly with ambiguous stares on their faces. "What are they thinking?" I wondered as I too watched quietly while taking note of the instructors' reliance on lecture peppered with an occasional question–answer sequence. As they talked, I had wished they would write down the names of the people and places they mentioned, and I wished for visuals, diagrams, timelines, anything to help me follow what they were talking about. So after the youth had left and Kelli asked for a quick debriefing because she wouldn't be able to attend the formal one, I was hopeful and curious.

Quickly and abruptly, she speaks: "I won't be here for our debriefing this afternoon so I want to say this now. There are kids who have separated themselves from the group, who are not very engaged. What I noticed from us was a lack of response; no one was reacting to it. The adults in back were chatting, which really sets a tone that you don't have to be listening. It is really important to model the behaviors we want them to do." "Good for you," I think, "they need to address their teaching strategies now." But Tim reacts defensively and is evidently agitated, and Marge echoes what he has tried to articulate: "I think we are all aware that we have certain speakers who stand out. If we stop to speak to kids who are not behaving it draws attention." And then it's lunchtime and the discussion is tabled till that afternoon.

After lunch, minus Kelli, they take up where they left off, and as I think back on it and consider its twists and turns, I realize that the talk they needed to have about the nature of their collaboration never occurred, and that the talk they did have would take center stage the rest of the week, but would never get openly addressed.

Tim starts off by apologizing for reacting so strongly to Kelli, but explains that if she had come up to him and asked to talk about her concern, he would have been less defensive. Frankie agrees, "Perhaps it would have been more appropriate for her to approach you rather than the larger group. It was your session and you had indeed seen the behavior she was referring to, and so [she] should have asked you about the seating." I am curious how others will react to Frankie's statement, which so clearly contradicts their mantra of open and shared deliberation, but Tim wants to say more. "There was a group of guys sitting over there and saying I'm not buying into what is going on here. I guess I want to allow more tolerance than Kelli. Although I was personally annoyed when one of the guys started to imitate what was being presented, and I decided that to go up to him would be very embarrassing to him." Nirman, a member of the national organization, who had been listening quietly, jumps in supportively: "You have far more patience than I do, during a camp I once led I had a kid cry because I called him on it. But then he was engaged. Some of us have different teaching styles. I didn't see what Kelli said as nonconstructive and destructive. I saw it as we could have kept the chatter in the back down, we were at fault. We can recognize that we have different teaching styles and help each other out."

I watch with hope this attempt to discuss the issue as one of teaching and one that could be solved collaboratively, but Tim, tensing up, builds instead on Nirman's handling of it as a disciplinary issue. "I would have not embarrassed to the extent that you would. I've seen you do it and you can pull it off. But I can't do that, I come off too strongly." And Imad, new to the team and a member of the national advocacy organization, offers a suggestion for handling the discipline: "Maybe the problem can be resolved through the camp counselors. I suggest that the counselors sit with the students and deal with that." And then Frankie voices a concern not yet raised: "Then we have the problem that the counselors may not have the training, and then there is the issue that they are all White and the children are all Black."

I groan quietly. "Yes, yes," I think. Although not the only Black students among the youth, the three teens being discussed are the most economically limited, so race and class play a role here, but this is not a disciplinary issue. This is a teaching issue, one of needing pedagogical strategies to reach out to different kinds of young people. After all, this is supposed to be a program for diversity and democracy. Could it be that these inner-city teens had never been to a camp before, or attended a history lecture with 26 other youth they did not know and who practice religions they may never have heard of? How were any of these young people supposed to figure out the norms of such a program overnight? But certainly someone in this group is going to see that and say something. And when Irene, a conflict resolution trainer and educator begins to speak, I listen. She is one of two Black faculty members and has years of experience handling discriminatory situations. "I'm listening on so many levels about race and culture. It is so hard as a White person to bring them in and there has to be a buy in, but I don't know. Why are they here?"

What Irene is asking is a question about expectations. What were the youths' expectations of this program? But Frankie takes it up as a failure in the adults' recruitment process and explains that some of the people who were sought out to identify appropriate teens for the program misinterpreted the point of the program and sent teenagers who don't fit "the model." Before anyone asks what this model looks like, the conversation becomes intense and difficult to follow, but the core of it is clearly an attempt to express solutions that reveal two opposing pedagogical philosophies: one view articulates a democratic pedagogy requiring adaptation and reaching out to the youth who have much to teach them; the other favors a transmission approach requiring receptivity from the youth who have much to learn.

Advocating for reaching out, Nirman draws on sociocultural theories that argue that one way to understand the inner-city Black youths' nonassimilatory patterns is by understanding how different behaviors are associated with different cultural norms. Frankie, however, who understands learning as transmission, worries that what she sees as asocial behavior will affect the behaviors of other students who are not acting out. Nellie, an associate with the camp who had been sitting quietly, tries to shift the focus to the program's responsibility toward the youth. "There seems to be two levels to this conversation. What kind of culture are we as faculty creating? What kind of culture do the youth create? What is the team doing to support the facilitation, what kind of culture do we want together? What kind of modeling do we want to do?" But her words fall on deaf ears as Tim seems beyond discussion: "Personally, I am not willing to tolerate anyone sabotaging this program. We have invested too much. Now if kids are having doubts that this is going to be a valuable experience, then ok. But if they are committed that this week is going to be a real drag, I am not willing to put up with that. So how are we going to deal with this? I'm thinking we need to tell the kids upfront this is what we think you are doing and we are not going to tolerate it. If this is what you are doing, there is an airplane waiting for you."

There is a quick discussion about behavior and race, some asking for patience, others agreeing with Tim, and then Nellie suggests that they let the youth develop their own community standards. "We need a little patience; we need a lot of vigilance. We see this over and over again, sometimes race, sometimes financial disparities. That's why I believe so strongly in community standards." And Frankie jumps on this as a solution: "If the students create a list of community standards they are going to buy in or they aren't going to buy in to them. But if they don't we can say if you are not working within that set of rules, you will be sent home." That said, the conversation is over, and I return to my cabin where Jude and Steve are waiting.

Discussion

This incident opened up multiple challenges for us as evaluators and as humans sharing a world with others. We were unsure where to begin or what issue needed most addressing. We were ashamed that a group of White liberals like ourselves could profess to support a diverse and democratic world and then reveal such classist, racist, and undemocratic perspectives. We understood that many of the statements made during this incident were the result of emotional and physical duress and fear that the program would fail; however, we were surprised by the group's inability to relate pedagogy to behavior, race, and class in this situation.

As it turned out, the youngsters stayed. Neither they nor any of the other teenagers ever again engaged in any behaviors considered problematic. Furthermore, all of the adults reached out to the youth in various interactive activities that succeeded, along with the youths' own efforts with each other, in building community. However, that first day set the pattern for the remainder of the week: each day had some hours of didactic presentation from adults, bookended with more interactive activities. Adult decision making likewise was set. Rather than clearly articulate and argue through their differing positions, the adults usually deferred to Frankie's final decision on the matter under discussion.

Our vignette illustrates the different layers of meanings present in most complex human interactions. In a separate publication (Freeman & Preissle, 2010) we pursue the pedagogical rift in the group between those assuming a transmissive model of education and those favoring a more transformative model of education. The rift divided the advocacy organization adults, who favored more didactic approaches to education from the camp adults and we three evaluators, who favored a more interactive approach. We believe that the adults' insistence on compliance to their transmissive efforts prevented them from more fully achieving their goal of promoting religious liberty in a democracy. In this chapter, however, we move our focus from pedagogy to the social dynamics in which we were ourselves complicit. These dynamics presented a democratic and inclusive façade that hid a more autocratic and hierarchical reality.

From the beginning the adults voiced the common goal of empowering youth leaders in the United States to defend and support religious freedoms, and they articulated a shared desire to reach out to diverse communities across the country. What never occurred was a deep consideration of how these diverse communities might enculturate youth to different models of leadership and how the program might adapt to these different forms of interaction.

Although deferring to Frankie to get things done, not everyone agreed with her perspective on whom and what the program was for. In our final focus group interviews with youth and adults, we believed we were getting the kind of diversity of opinion we needed for our report to push the program founders to recognize and reflect on their own levels of acceptance and resistance to the diversity of experience the youth brought. This was a highlight of our assessment. We were stunned, therefore, to later learn how the differences in adult perspectives were addressed: the National Advocacy Organization separated itself from the Liberal Religious Camp and continued the program on its own under Frankie's leadership. In our concluding sections we offer reflections on how our responsiveness could have been more critical.

Moral Knowledge, or, What We Did, or Failed to Do, and Why

An ongoing issue for naturalistic or responsive evaluators concerns the many roles evaluators find themselves taking in the course of an evaluation. Working with stakeholders is a relational, situational, and personal endeavor and involves sensitivity to the emotional, psychological, and social well-being of a diversity of people, while also pressing them to share information that may be at odds with others with whom they also have personal relationships. It involves, in other words, moral knowledge. Moral knowledge involves our capacity to judge when a response or action is called for in a particular situation, what that response should be, and the consequences, positive or negative, of the action or response (Connor, 1999).

One of the strong prejudices we brought to the evaluation is a commitment to the value of dialogue. We agree with Abma (2006) that the conditions for "good" dialogue involve "the willingness of stakeholders to participate, to share power, to change in the process, and to be open and respectful" (p. 34). What we struggled with was helping ensure that "good" dialogue occurred while not disempowering the group's process by stepping in and taking it over. In hindsight, we believe that we mistook the locus of our concern. For example, one reason we did not intervene in the conversation was out of respect for the group's own desire for deliberative dialogue and the false belief that intervening in their process would be disempowering to them. We believed in their capacities for development because of how they did confront each other, speak their own minds, uncover the values underneath them, express anxiety, anger, and frustration one minute and reach out, voicing their care and commitment to each other and to their shared vision the next. Who were we, we thought, to step in and judge the quality of their interactions or predict their outcomes? Furthermore, when we did participate in the dialogue to offer our perspective on what we were hearing, our voices merely blended in as one point of view among 20 others. Our solution was to work from these deliberations and build in constructivist procedures to elicit further stakeholder perspectives on practices we felt fell short of their ideals of democracy and diversity and recirculate those perspectives in individual interviews and focus groups. What we realize now was that our inability to resolve how to integrate ourselves into their deliberative process and intervene in the dialogic encounters themselves meant that our actions, or inactions in this case, reinforced some of the patterns of which we were so critical.

Our biggest failure, therefore, was not directly addressing the issue of power and how power, especially Frankie's, halted deliberation of key issues. Not alone in this view, one founding member described her disappointment in the inability of the adults to work more collaboratively. "I think there was a lack of clarity around who was effectively in charge . . . . The way it was described to me, it was a collaboration between [different groups], and I think [instead] there were power struggles. . . . Everyone who was involved followed Frankie's lead and I think we followed her lead for different reasons, all of them not necessarily admirable."

Dealing with power inequalities as they were occurring would have required someone to call on a stronger democratic process and take the leadership in developing and putting into practice a critical pedagogy that would involve us all. The decision of who would take that leadership need not have been ours to make, but we were in as good a position as others to recommend such an action. We knew alliances were being formed between some members of the group, and we witnessed, just as everyone did, how some viewpoints were being excluded. Power differentials were never addressed by us, or anyone else, during implementation. By not adequately responding to the founding team's desire for input on their collaborative process and actively informing that process, we failed our stakeholders, especially those who found themselves silenced in the group's process.

Moral Discourse, or, What We Might Have Done Differently

Moral discourse involves paying attention to how we think, talk, act, and call on moral frameworks within everyday practice such as evaluation. As participants proceed with their activities, evaluators engage them in contemplative discourse about the priorities and values underlying program practices and stakeholder perspectives, and analysis of the language used becomes a source of information about self and others (MacIntyre, 1984; Schwandt, 1989, 2002). When we collect stakeholder perspectives and experiences during an evaluation, we are collecting bits and pieces of this moral discourse—what people connected to a program value about it and wish to achieve. In promoting a collaborative approach, the program founders tried to keep such a discourse open but failed, as we also failed in assisting them. Although a critical approach does not seek to proffer or impose a solution, how might we have worked out a better integration of what we could offer this group without taking over their process? How might we have integrated such a discourse into our practice?

When we conduct an evaluation, we are putting into play our beliefs about knowledge generation, learning, and transformation. An ethical conflict for us was sensing that we were acting in ways contrary to our own beliefs about these things. There are two pieces we now consider to be essential to the resolution of the conflicts we experienced. The first is making clear to our client our position on the issues as they arise for us. If we are to be members of a formative team, we must reflect on and make explicit how our own values are guiding our engagement. The second follows from the first. As outsiders to a program we are in a special position to articulate opposing stakeholder values as we hear and observe them and to inform the group of how their practices, whether during development or implementation, are favoring or discriminating against these values.

Using the issues raised in the vignette for reflective purposes, how might we have acted differently in this and other situations? It is easier to speak critically of the acts of others than it is to acknowledge how quickly we too can (and do) fall into racist discourses. Rather than consider reflectively how we could assist the founders in strengthening their process, we reacted emotionally to their transitory panic and talk of exclusion. This resulted in our focusing primarily on understanding the perspectives that divided the group at the expense of probing into their collaboration, or lack thereof. What might have happened if we had pointed out that their reaction to the youths' seeming disengagement was likely being distorted by prevalent stereotypes of Blacks and behavior? How might this conversation have led them to better understand how their fears about behavior and the possibility of having their own views challenged coincided with their disagreement over whom their program was intended for? Finally, how might this conversation help those who preferred a transmissive pedagogy better understand how transformational pedagogies help address issues of engagement through teaching rather than discipline? Rather than engage them in better understanding the effects of stereotypical thinking and assist them in their efforts to work against it, we too balked, and allowed our shock and discomfort to interfere with clear thinking about our responsibilities.

Responsibility for General and Public Welfare, or, Prioritizing Our Commitments

Looking back over our evaluation, we believe there were many areas in which we were successful. We developed strong relationships with all the program stakeholders, even the ones we disagreed with. We presented their perspectives on the strengths and weaknesses of the program in a fair and comprehensive way. We paid attention to how the youth were being treated and how they benefited from the program and were pleased to be able to report positively on both accounts. During implementation the adults never mistreated the teenagers or discriminated against them personally. Although the conflict represented in the vignette could be understood as an expression of the founders' fears at being ill-prepared for a diversity of youth broader than they had anticipated, it was also an expression of their understanding of how they believed their program ought to be designed so as to benefit society. Our critical retrospection, in that it is critical of the elitist view espoused by some of the founders, is our expression of how we believe programs and practices such as these ought to benefit society.

What we understand now in retrospect was how the differences in pedagogical preferences represented differences in how program founders understood the responsibility of the program to the client. In our view and the view

NEW DIRECTIONS FOR EVALUATION • DOI: 10.1002/ev

of those who professed a transformative pedagogy, the youth were the program's client. The program should provide a rich educational experience that would transform the youths' understanding of their own capacities for empathy, advocacy, and action and allow them to contribute to their communities and society in their own way. Frankie and others who supported her view believed the client to be the mission of the national organization. In this view, you do not turn to youth for understanding and guidance because you already know what the mission is. The youth are an abstraction. They are the future of a nation, and as such it is the nation that the program takes to be its client. Had we reflected more critically on AEA's principle of responsibility for general and public welfare, we might have been in a better position to help the program founders understand that their disagreement was in how they interpreted their responsibilities to society. Moving the discourse away from pedagogy to one of civil society, a discourse all the founders were well versed in, might have greatly assisted their process.

Understanding how we interpret our responsibility to society is crucial to understanding how to guide our actions as program evaluators. In the end, we overlooked opportunities for deliberative discourse and we stayed silent while Frankie enacted a business model of collaboration where one leader solicits everyone's input, but then individually makes a final decision, and where leadership itself is assumed to be based on meritorious and elitist criteria. We now know we were enchanted by the active and dialogic, albeit ineffectual, engagement of our stakeholders, swayed by our own advocacy for their mission, and diverted by our concern for them as individuals from our commitment to a democratic society. We hope that by making visible what are very common, but difficult to address, occurrences and conversations in diversity-oriented programs, our story contributes to the impressive work in evaluation that supports dialogue, deliberation, diversity, and a democratic society, as well as programs like the one we evaluated, that seek ways to foster these values.

Acknowledgments

We would like to thank the youth and adults for their participation in this evaluation study and for their commitment to creating a better world. Thanks are also due to Kathryn Roulston and Jodi Kaufmann for feedback on earlier versions of this chapter. Finally, we are grateful for the funding we received from the University of Georgia and the unnamed nonprofit organization.

References

Abma, T. A. (2006). The practice and politics of responsive evaluation. *American Journal of Evaluation, 27*(1), 31–43.
American Evaluation Association (AEA). (2004). *American Evaluation Association guiding principles for evaluators.* Fairhaven, MA: Author.

Beiner, R. (1983). *Political judgment*. Chicago: University of Chicago Press.
Connor, W. R. (1999). Moral knowledge in the modern university. *Ideas*, 6(1). Retrieved October 3, 2007, from http//:nationalhumanitiescenter.org/ideasv6n1/connormoral.htm
Erickson, F. (1986). Qualitative methods in research on teaching. In M. C. Witrock (Ed.), *Handbook of research on teaching* (3rd ed., pp. 119–161). New York: Macmillan.
Freeman, M., & Preissle, J. (2010, July-August). Pedagogical ethical dilemmas in a responsive evaluation of a leadership program for youth. *The International Journal of Qualitative Studies in Education*, 23(4), 463–478.
Greene, J. C., & Abma, T. A. (Eds.). (2001). *Responsive evaluation. New Directions for Evaluation*, 92.
Humphreys, M. (2005). Getting personal: Reflexivity and autoethnographic vignettes. *Qualitative Inquiry*, 11(6), 840–860.
Macbeth, D. (2001). On "reflexivity" in qualitative research: Two readings and a third. *Qualitative Inquiry*, 7(1), 35–68.
MacIntyre, A. (1984). *After virtue: A study in moral theory* (2nd ed.). Notre Dame, IN: University of Notre Dame Press.
Polkinghorne, D. E. (1995). Narrative configuration in qualitative analysis. *Qualitative Studies in Education*, 8(1), 5–23.
Schwandt, T. A. (1989). Recapturing moral discourse in evaluation. *Educational Researcher*, 18(8), 11–16.
Schwandt, T. A. (2002). *Evaluation practice reconsidered*. New York: Peter Lang.
Schwandt, T.A. (2007). On the importance of revisiting the study of ethics in evaluation. In S. Kushner & N. Norris (Eds.), *Dilemmas of engagement: Evaluation and the new public management. Advances in program evaluation* (Vol. 10, pp. 117–127). Amsterdam: Elsevier JAI.
Segerholm, C. (2003). Researching evaluation in national (state) politics and administration: A critical approach. *The American Journal of Evaluation*, 24(3), 353–372.

MELISSA FREEMAN *is associate professor of qualitative research methodologies in the College of Education at the University of Georgia; her research focuses on critical, hermeneutic, and relational approaches to educational research and evaluation.*

JUDITH PREISSLE *is the 2001 Distinguished Aderhold Professor in the College of Education, University of Georgia, and an affiliated faculty member of UGA's Institute for Women's Studies. She teaches, researches, and writes in educational anthropology, qualitative research, feminist studies, and ethics.*

STEVEN HAVICK *is a doctoral candidate in the University of Georgia's Department of Elementary and Social Studies Education and currently teaches U.S. history at Salem High School outside of Atlanta.*

NEW DIRECTIONS FOR EVALUATION • DOI: 10.1002/ev

Segerholm, C. (2010). Examining outcomes-based educational evaluation through a critical theory lens. In M. Freeman (Ed.), *Critical social theory and evaluation practice. New
Directions for Evaluation, 127,* 59–69.

5

Examining Outcomes-Based Educational Evaluation Through a Critical Theory Lens

Christina Segerholm

Abstract

*Contemporary educational evaluation policy and practice can be challenged by
applying critical theory and hermeneutics perspectives in evaluation and by asking whose interests are being served through evaluation. Using educational evaluation in Sweden as the context, the author argues for an explanation-oriented
evaluation approach that assumes education is complex, multilayered, and
infused with conflicting interests and intentions. The author concludes that evaluations that attend to this complexity have the potential to influence educational
policy significantly.* © Wiley Periodicals, Inc., and the American Evaluation
Association.

Today education policy is not only an issue for nation states, but also
of interest to organizations like the Organization for Economic Co-
Operation and Development (OECD), the United Nations Educational, Scientific and Cultural Organization (UNESCO), and the European
Union (EU). Even though these organizations differ in their aims and in
their constitutional power in relation to member nations, they all attempt
to make education a means for increasing competitiveness on the global
market (Ozga, Seddon, & Popkewitz, 2006). This is done through conscious policy-making efforts, anchored in human-capital theory and the idea

of competition (Robertson, 2005). It is also done through evaluative activities like quality assurance, assessment, and international tests like PISA and TIMMS that are used to measure and compare specific educational outcomes in different nation states. Furthermore, it is likely that one reason for this fascination with outcome measures in education is the prevailing doctrine of "governing by objectives and results" (other concepts used are governing by targets/goals and results/outcomes) (Porter, 1996; Segerholm, 2007).

This governing doctrine rests on a rationale in which clear objectives (goals/targets) for education are set in advance, and education results (outcomes) are measured by comparing the results to the objectives. This is commonly done through the aggregation of test results from individual students. Evaluation of education quality is then based on a comparison between the objectives and the aggregated individual student results. Through comparisons of results between nations, the idea is that competition is sustained, thus leading to improvement by borrowing policy from nations that are doing well in these international endeavors. The same rationale is often used within nation states, regions, and cities/municipalities to stimulate local improvement. However, tests and outcome measures do not adequately portray education or educational processes precisely because they lack information about didactic and pedagogical issues (process information). For evaluations to be able to inform education policy and practice there is also a need to take preconditions for education and context into account. Concentrating on educational outcomes only answers questions about what the results of education are. If these results are compared to preset objectives, goals, or standards, it is also possible to assess attainment levels. However, to understand or explain outcomes require more complex evaluation approaches that incorporate context and process information. In order to inform policy and practice, reasons for particular outcomes/results must be identified, and that can only be achieved through analysis of the relations between preconditions/context, how the evaluand is carried out, and the outcomes/results/impact of the evaluand.

Given the portrayals of the contemporary educational context and educational evaluation outlined above, how might a critical perspective inform educational evaluation policy and practice? How would it shape evaluation design and analysis? The aim of the article is to answer these questions. Specifically, I will: (a) offer a critical analysis of the reliance of outcomes-based measures in educational evaluation in national and international contexts, (b) provide an overview of how critical theory and hermeneutics challenge the taken-for-granted assumptions currently guiding educational evaluation, (c) provide an alternative conception of educational evaluation based on critical theory and hermeneutics, and (d) describe what this alternative evaluation approach would offer education using Sweden as an example.

NEW DIRECTIONS FOR EVALUATION • DOI: 10.1002/ev

A Critical Analysis of Educational Evaluation

In 1972 a group of scholars met in Cambridge to explore alternative ways of conducting evaluations. They were concerned that the then rapidly expanding evaluation activities in education were not "accompanied by an equivalent surge of new thinking about either evaluation methods or their usefulness for decision-making" (MacDonald & Parlett, 1973, p. 74). It is instructive to recall what kind of evaluation they were criticizing.

> This model of evaluation stemmed from a long-established and securely rooted tradition of educational measurement on both sides of the Atlantic. . . . Federal policy makers demanded of educational innovators that they both pre-specified the intended performance gains and provided subsequent proof of "pay-off". Despite mounting criticisms of the engineering-type assumptions of such "pre-ordinate" evaluation, and the tentative emergence of alternative approaches, the model was still serviceable enough to be exported to [Britain]. (MacDonald & Parlett, 1973, p. 75, footnotes in original omitted)

Furthermore, this group of scholars explained that this kind of evaluation did not work. The practical as well as theoretical problems inherent in measuring preset objectives were hard to overcome and reduced the utility of the measures. To be of value to educators and policy makers, they proposed more varied educational evaluation approaches that were sensitive to context, took into consideration program histories, included instructional and learning processes, and considered as a starting point more complex and overarching purposes of education (MacDonald & Parlett, 1973).

More than 35 years have passed since this "Cambridge manifesto" was published. Several evaluation approaches and models have been developed to represent educational processes and outcomes better and to benefit practitioners, policy makers, students, and other stakeholders. However, as noted above, we are again, globally, in a period when educational evaluation has become more and more a question of measuring outcomes (now called *quality*) in relation to preset objectives, and tests are again the favored model of doing this. The consequences of testing have changed little since the 1970s. Critics then and now argue that the overreliance on tests and outcomes-based evaluations lead to distortions at all levels (teach-to-the-test, window dressing, manipulation of data, and so on). (See, for example, Linn, 2002, and Nichols & Berliner, 2007.) Another consequence of testing is that teachers and education bureaucrats tend to spend a vast amount of time administering these tests and composing quality statements to engage in quality assessment and assurance systems ("Fabricating," 2009). This obsession with measuring quality (outcomes compared to preset goals) has led policy makers in education to concentrate more on policies of evaluation and quality assurance than policy about the purpose and context of education (Lundgren, 2006, pp. 11–12). In turn this orientation to policy-making means that education is now also governed by evaluative activities (evaluation and quality-assurance systems), a form of governing from behind (Segerholm, 2009), moving the discussion further away from policies that emanate from an interest in what kind of people and society education is to foster. International and transnational organizations (for example, the OECD and the EU) are actively promoting these evaluation and quality-assurance policies and practices in education, and this is partly done through policy elites (government officers, evaluators, researchers) taking part in policy-setting activities and international test programs (Lawn & Lingard, 2002; see also Bourdieu, 1999).

A Critical Theory Perspective

Critical theory goes back to the Frankfurt school, where social science researchers aimed to understand the totality of societies by combining theories of analysis of societies with theories of analysis of the individual (Burill, 1987, p. 11). In developing a conceptual framework that brings critical theory, hermeneutics, and educational evaluation together, I draw from more recent work that has critically analyzed and connected social, economic, and power dimensions of contemporary societies to individuals' positions, identities, sense-making, and practices in education (Ball, 1994; Bernstein, 1996; Bourdieu, 1988; Schwandt, 2002). A common denominator for these scholars is an interest in always asking, "Whose interests are being served?" (Schwandt, 1997). A heritage from the older critical theory tradition is the ambition to stay independent of hegemonic discourses/ideologies, and of powerful interests, be they the state, private enterprises, or other groups or organizational interests. This critical stance in research is value laden and directs inquiry and research questions in certain directions; it is thus also related to evaluation, as evaluation is inherently concerned with values and valuation (House & Howe, 1999).

A critical perspective is directly related to the "path to knowledge," that is, how we come to know something about the world and ourselves. We understand the world around us by interpretation. We form our understandings from more or less explicit, conscious, and already existing perceptions and conceptions, what in the hermeneutical tradition are called *preunderstandings*. There can be no one-to-one relationship between our understanding and the world (Alvesson & Sköldberg, 2000). Coming to understand something in a deeper or more complex way entails challenging one's preunderstandings and taken-for-granted, commonsense understandings. The relation between parts and totality of a phenomenon (or text) and how this interrelationship helps us understand the totality as more than the sum of the parts, and each part's relation to each other and to the totality, is a hermeneutical cornerstone that is useful in understanding education as a complex, historically, socially, politically, and culturally situated enterprise. Evaluation of education therefore needs to take both totality and parts and the relation between them into the process of coming to understand. Stake's (1995) case-study approach has much to offer in that respect. Coming to understand the world in a different fashion and unveil hidden values, ideas, and powers entails interpretation and the construction of new understanding; this search for patterns under the surface and attempts to represent these findings to others has been labeled *critical hermeneutics* (Ödman, 2007; Ricoeur, 1993).

Using a critical theory perspective in educational evaluation has less to do with picking the right theorist's view than it does cultivating curiosity and an inquiring stance that includes questions about:

- The history and power relations of the evaluand;
- The political agenda of different actors and the underlying ideology of the evaluand;
- Conceptions of what it means to be human, what is judged to be a "good" society, and which values are at stake;
- How social structures and identities in society are sustained and actively supported, and who gains and who loses;
- What evaluation does in relation to these questions; and finally
- How an evaluation is to be carried out given the particular conditions in a specific commission.

An Alternative Conception for Educational Evaluation: Explanation-Oriented or Theory-Oriented Evaluation

How could the design and analysis of educational evaluation be conceived through a critical theorist's lens? One attempt was made in the middle and end of the 1970s in Sweden to craft an evaluation approach that applied a critical perspective and started with a view of education as complex, multilayered, and infused with conflicting interests and intentions. Inspired by the Cambridge manifesto of 1973, this effort was one among many at that time criticizing what was viewed as a simplistic notion of educational evaluation as equal to measurement of individual student's test results. However, there was also a concern that process evaluation approaches at that time were too subjective and did not take into consideration broader theories of education and power relations in society.

Setting out to design an evaluation approach that could more appropriately capture educational processes based on research, and also incorporate a critical perspective, Franke-Wikberg and Johansson (1975) developed the embryo to explanation-oriented or theory-oriented evaluation. *Explanation* denotes the ambition to seek understanding based on contextual and historic explanations rather than causal explanations. That is also the reason why *theory-oriented* was used as an alternative label to this approach. *Theory* implies the explicit use of theories of education to understand relations between preconditions, process, and outcomes (see further below).

This approach was later elaborated upon and more strongly formulated by Franke-Wikberg and Lundgren (1980).

One of the aims of the approach was to provide more useful explanations and understandings of the outcome of education as a basis for change. In order to do this it was necessary to incorporate information of (a) preconditions of education (a reform, program, project, or network) including its historical, social (and geographical in my interpretation of this approach) situatedness; (b) the educational process, that is, how the program was carried out; and (c) the outcomes of education/the program. Dahllöf (1967) paved the way for this approach in his study of how preconditions, like amount of time, co-varied with instruction and outcomes, the frame-factor theory developed further by Lundgren. The explanation-oriented evaluation approach not only stressed the importance of the relation between context, process, and outcomes, but also underlined the need for a thorough understanding of the relation between formal education and power relations in society and the state. "What purposes does education serve and for whom?" was asked, instead of normative and policy-oriented questions like, "What purposes should education serve?"

To ask what purposes education serves and for whom opens possibilities for a critical perspective on education without leading to prescriptions of what is good for the individual and society. Such a question also points to the necessity of viewing education as part of a particular historical, political, economical, geographical, and social context. In explanation-oriented evaluation, the evaluator needs to spell out his or her theoretical understanding of education and the particular evaluand, and in so doing try to describe his or her preunderstandings. This notion should, however, be challenged by the interaction with the information collected throughout the evaluation process so that new understandings are achieved. The critical hermeneutical perspective is visible in this position by its engagement with context; its pronounced interest in underlying assumptions and ideologies in programs and education reforms; its reliance on sociological knowledge, meaning that power and social positions are unequally distributed; its ambition to understand education programs/reforms/projects in new ways; and its recognition of knowledge as provisional, and the path to knowledge as an act of interpretation and construction.

This approach shares some similarities with the theory-driven approach of Rossi and Freeman (1985) and with the conceptual framework presented by realist evaluators Mark, Henry, and Julnes (1999) and Pawson and Tilly (1997). However, explanation-oriented evaluation is interested in power relations in a society as they are laid down in education, which is not an explicit knowledge orientation in theory-driven or realist evaluation. How strong this interest in power relations is expressed in individual evaluations carried out using the explanation-oriented approach varies, because many of its original time-specific ideas have undergone revisions and changes. It is also a rather demanding approach in its information collecting and analysis ambitions, often leading to a narrowing of the design for practical and resource reasons.

To conclude the description of this critical evaluation approach, the suggestion is that an analysis of the evaluand and its context has to be done before a decision on design and analysis is made. No particular evaluation method or analysis fit all evaluands and contexts when there is a concern about coming to new understandings or about social justice. This collides with many evaluation commissions when requests for proposals have to be answered with little knowledge required to make informed evaluation decisions, and also when resources in the commission are restricted. Furthermore, it is not always desirable to carry out an action-oriented and/or dialogic evaluation, because the power balance in the program (or network or reform) may in fact be so skewed that less powerful actors/stakeholders are overrun in such processes. (See, for example, the Greene, 2000, account of problems encountered when practicing deliberate democratic evaluation.) The overarching concern is to try to respond to the types of critical questions posed in the above section, and always ask whose interests are being served by the program and by the evaluation. The responsibility of the evaluator first and foremost is the evaluation and its practice and impacts, not the evaluand and its practices and policies, although the line in between is sometimes hard to draw.

The following example may help to illustrate the arguments put forward. In an evaluation of a national initiative on local development work to promote increased awareness of the importance of recognizing ethnic diversity in educational and pedagogical processes in order to increase attainment, an assessment of the impact of the initiative at individual and local levels was requested. The commissioner of the (then) National Agency for School Development, asked initially: How did the particular school or municipality implement the initiative? Did ethnic minority students perform better as a result of the initiative? In negotiating the evaluation design it was suggested that in order to understand the implementation and possible impacts it was also necessary to ask about the national agency's policy and work in designing and carrying out the initiative (involving the dissemination of extra resources to municipalities and schools), because that inevitably set conditions for who got the resources and on what grounds (i.e., what the agency accepted as good pedagogical work concerning ethnic minorities). Information was therefore collected concerning the agency's criteria for getting the extra resources, for the process of selection and distribution, and for following up with the local projects that got money. One of the results of the evaluation was a realization that a very strong strand of implementation of the present governing logic, governing by goals and results, was embedded in the national agency's way of handling the initiative. Ideas of understanding ethnic diversity in educational processes were less present. There was also an initial expectation of measuring individual student results, which was not reasonable considering the short period of time the initiative had been running. This expectation also turned out to be less helpful in local settings, because the situations for ethnic minority students who were part of the initiative more often concerned attendance and social behavior in the classrooms than attainment. One answer to the question of whose interests were being served by this national initiative was therefore "the state and its civil servants" in the ambitions to strengthen the contemporary governing principle. Educational content matters, apart from language acquisition, were less prominent. These evaluation results (there were others as well) made it possible for the civil servants to reflect and change design in future national initiatives should they decide that the governing principle was of less importance than some other directions.

Contemporary Context of Educational Evaluation Revisited: Explanation and Understanding Versus Outcome and Quality

Returning to the contemporary context of educational evaluation laid out in the introduction, this final section provides a discussion of how the critical evaluation approach described above may help to elucidate the role of evaluation in education policy; that is, what role might evaluation and evaluators take? This discussion relates to the critical theory tradition of self-reflection and self-criticism and uses Sweden as an example.

Starting with a very brief description of the context, or preconditions for contemporary evaluative activities in compulsory education in Sweden, it can be said that an incremental change from rule-based governing to governing by goals and results took place starting at the end of the 1970s. Likewise, an incremental increase of different evaluative activities followed this restructuring (Segerholm, 2009). For several decades Sweden has also been an active part of the development of international tests like PISA, and from 1995 its membership in the EU has increased this international involvement in global education policy. The EU's work on indicators for education quality, lifelong learning, and learning to learn are good examples of the interaction between the EU and Swedish education policy making (Grek et al., 2009).

Today educational evaluation, or rather evaluative activities in education in Sweden, form a web of interrelated activities and processes (Segerholm, 2005, 2009). The Education Act and other regulations require a whole range of activities to be carried out. Information mainly about educational outcomes is collected en masse and in accordance with a rationale much like the one laid out in the explanation-directed approach, such as it was developed for local development purposes (Franke-Wikberg, 1990). National inspections every third year in all schools and municipalities, annual municipal quality accounts, individual school quality accounts, yearly follow-up statistics, national tests, international tests (PISA, TIMMS, PEARLS, etc.), and annual individual development plans for all students based on an evaluation of their achievements are required evaluative activities. On top of that, teachers, principals, local politicians, and administrators may want to have other evaluations of particular local efforts carried out. This mass activity, evaluating education at all levels, impacts education practice in ways that are not always spelled out or planned. It is safe to say that they are intended to form a part of the governing of education in Sweden. This means that they are not only about making value judgments of the existing education system, but are also steering future educational systems. In all these activities education researchers and evaluators are active either as proponents of particular models, as designers of tests, as designers or experts to formal policy-makers' reform missions, or as carriers/brokers of evaluation ideas (policy) in international settings (foreign-aid missions, for example). In Sweden these activities are now so overwhelming that teachers have recently filed a complaint (in June 2009) concerning their work situation, claiming that they are overburdened with tasks related to quality work and evaluation, keeping them from engaging seriously in teaching ("Skolvärlden," 2009; "Stressade Lärare," 2009). As evaluators in education we are part of this situation, both the overload of evaluative activities and the quality turn (ideology) in education. We are also policy makers when we ordinate, design, and carry out tests, evaluations, and quality assurance systems, albeit never accountable to the public. The situation today, at least in Sweden, and from what I know of other education systems, is quite similar to what the scholars gathered in Cambridge in 1972 worried about. The difference is that today's systems are even more comprehensive, use technologies (like self-evaluation and sometimes dialogue) that go into "peoples souls" [sic] (Ball, 2003), support an instrumental, technological view of education, and rely on a governing rationale (governing by goals and results), that was outmoded in 1989 when the former Soviet Union broke down, all in the hope of promoting competitiveness on the global market.

By applying the critical perspective laid out in the explanation-oriented evaluation approach, using today's evaluation practices and policies in Sweden as an example and situating them in a global context, it is hoped that policy makers and practitioners may make more informed decisions about future evaluative activities, asking questions like: Whose interests are being served in the evaluated education program and by the evaluation? What notions/policies of education are supported in the education program and by the proposed evaluation? More arguments for the applicability of a critical perspective can be found in the new Cambridge manifesto that was crafted in a sixth conference in 2004 (Elliott & Kushner, 2007) as a consequence of the identified pathologies in today's educational policy-making and evaluation exercises.

Acknowledgments

I would like to thank Melissa Freeman for invaluable critique and good suggestions in structuring this chapter. My thanks also to Gordon Hoke for friendly support and encouragement.

References

Alvesson, M., & Sköldberg, K. (2000). *Reflexive methodology: New vistas for qualitative research*. London: Sage.

Ball, S. J. (1994). *Education reform: A critical and post-structural approach*. Buckingham, UK: Open University Press.

Ball, S. J. (2003). The teacher's soul and the terrors of performativity. *Journal of Education Policy, 18*(2), 215–228.

Bernstein, B. (1996). *Pedagogy, symbolic control and identity: Theory, research, critique*. London: Taylor & Francis.

Bourdieu, P. (1988). *Homo academius*. Oxford, UK: Polity Press.

Bourdieu, P. (1999). The social conditions of the international circulation of ideas. In R. Shusterman (Ed.), *Bourdieu: A critical reader* (pp. 220–228). Oxford, UK: Blackwell.

Burill, J. (Ed.) (1987). *Kritisk teori—En introduktion* [Critical theory—An introduction] Göteborg, Sweden: Daidalos.

Dahllöf, U. (1967). *Skoldifferentiering och undervisningsförlopp* [School differentiation and the teaching process] (Doctoral thesis). *Göteborg Studies in Educational Sciences* (Vol. 2). Stockholm: Almqvist & Wiksell.

Elliott, J., & Kushner, S. (2007). The need for a manifesto for educational programme evaluation. *Cambridge Journal of Education, 37*(3), 321–336.

Fabricating Quality: Data and the New Governanace of Education [Special issue]. (2009). *Journal of Education Policy, 24*(2).

Franke-Wikberg, S. (1990). *En strategi för utvärdering och lokal utveckling av utbildningskvalitet* [A strategy for evaluation and local development of educational quality] (Working paper No. 81). Umeå, Sweden: Umeå University, Department of Education.

Franke-Wikberg, S., & Johansson, M. (1975). *Utvärdering av undervisning. En problemanalys och några empiriska studier på universitetsnivå* [Evaluation of education and instruction. An analysis of the problem and some empirical studies at university level]. Doctoral thesis, Umeå University, Department of Education, Umeå, Sweden.

Franke-Wikberg, S., & Lundgren, U. P. (1980). *Att värdera utbildning. Del 1.* [To evaluate education. Part 1.] Stockholm: Wahlström & Widstrand.

Greene, J. (2000). Challenges in practicing deliberative democratic evaluation. In K. E. Ryan & L. DeStefano (Eds.), *Evaluation as a democratic process: Promoting inclusion, dialogue, and deliberation. New Directions for Evaluation, 85*, 13–26.

Grek, S., Lawn, M., Lingard, B., Ozga, J., Rinne, R., Segerholm, C., et al. (2009). National policy brokering and the construction of the European education space in England, Sweden, Finland and Scotland. *Comparative Education, 45*(1), 5–21.

House, E. R., & Howe, K. R. (1999). *Values in evaluation and social research*. Thousand Oaks, CA: Sage.

Lawn, M., & Lingard, B. (2002). Constructing a European policy space in educational governance: The role of transnational policy actors. *European Educational Research Journal, 1*(2), 290–307.

Linn, R. L. (2002). Assessments and accountability. *Educational Researcher, 29*(2), 4–16.

Lundgren, U. P. (2006). Political governing and curriculum change—From active to reactive curriculum reforms. The need for reorientation of curriculum theory. *Studies in Educational Policy and Educational Philosophy 1*. Retrieved from http://www.upi.artisan.se

MacDonald, B., & Parlett, M. (1973). Rethinking evaluation: Notes from the Cambridge Conference. *Cambridge Journal of Education, 3*(2), 74–81.

Mark, M., Henry, G. T., & Julnes, G. (1999). Towards an integrative framework for evaluation practice. *American Journal of Evaluation, 20*, 177–198.

Nichols, S. L., & Berliner, D. C. (2007). *Collateral damage: How high-stakes testing corrupts America's schools*. Cambridge, MA: Harvard Education Press.

Ödman, P. J. (2007). *Tolkning, förståelse, vetande. Hermeneutik i teori och praktik* (2nd ed.). [Interpretation, understanding and knowing: The theory and practice of hermeneutics (2nd ed.)]. Stockholm: Norstedts akademiska förlag.

Ozga, J., Seddon, T., & Popkewitz, T. S. (2006). Introduction. Education research and policy: Steering the knowledge-based economy. In J. Ozga, T. Seddon, & T. S. Popkewitz (Eds.). *Education research and policy. Steering the knowledge-based economy* (pp. 1–14). London: Routledge.

Pawson, R., & Tilly, N. (1997). *Realistic evaluation.* London: Sage.

Porter, T. M. (1996). *Trust in numbers: The pursuit of objectivity in science and public life.* Princeton, NJ: Princeton University Press.

Ricoeur, P. (1993). *Från text till handling. En antologi om hermeneutik* (4th ed.) [From text to action. An anthology on hermeneutics (4th ed.)]. Stockholm: Symposion.

Robertson, S. L. (2005). Re-imagining and rescripting the future of education: Global knowledge economy discourses and the challenge to education systems. *Comparative Education, 41*(2), 151–170.

Rossi, P. H., & Freeman, H. E. (1985). *Evaluation: A systematic approach* (3rd ed.). Beverly Hills, CA: Sage.

Schwandt, T. A. (1997). Whose interests are being served? Program evaluation as a conceptual practice of power. In L. Mabry (Ed.), *Evaluation and the postmodern dilemma. Advances in Program Evaluation, 3,* 89–104.

Schwandt, T. A. (2002). *Evaluation practice reconsidered.* New York: Peter Lang.

Segerholm, C. (2005, October). *Coping with evaluations: Influences of evaluative systems on school-organizations in four Swedish municipalities.* Paper presented at the AEA/CES conference, Toronto, Canada.

Segerholm, C. (2007). New public management and evaluation under decentralizing regimes in education. In S. Kushner & C. Pollitt (Eds.), *Dilemmas of engagement: Evaluation and the new public management. Advances in Program Evaluation, 10,* 129–138.

Segerholm, C. (2009). "We are doing well on QAE": The case of Sweden. *Journal of Education Policy, 24*(2), 195–209.

Skolvärlden måste bli modernare; Vi på friskolor vågar inte ens knysta [Schools must be more modern; At independent schools no one dares say a word]. (2009, May 30). *Dagens Nyheter,* p. 18.

Stake, R. E. (1995). *The art of case study research.* Thousand Oaks, CA: Sage.

Stressade lärare anmäler omöjlig arbetssituation [Teachers under stress file a complaint concerning their impossible work situation]. (2009, May 27). *Dagens Nyheter,* p. 14.

CHRISTINA SEGERHOLM is professor in education at Mid Sweden University.

6

Against the Majoritarian Story of School Reform: The Comer Schools Evaluation as a Critical Race Counternarrative

George W. Noblit, Michelle Jay

Abstract

Critical race theory (CRT) is a relatively new theory that has been little used in evaluation practice. The authors explore an example of critical race evaluation working with James Comer's School Development Program. In this evaluation common tropes associated with CRT were used to construct a counternarrative of school reform. The authors conclude that CRT has a place in evaluation, but that it also makes some demands on evaluators and those being evaluated that may make it less likely to be used than other theories. © Wiley Periodicals, Inc., and the American Evaluation Association.

As Freeman and Vasconcelos (this issue) argue, critical approaches are best thought of in terms of specific groups engaged with specific issues. Given this, one would suppose that evaluation would be a natural arena for critical studies. However, our experience has been that those who seek our services as evaluators are put off by the notion of critical evaluation. In part, this is because clients are worried that the critique will be applied to them, and thus are more interested in a kinder, gentler version of evaluation. Clearly though, when evaluations are required by funders or other sponsors, they are likely to desire a more critical approach.

NEW DIRECTIONS FOR EVALUATION, no. 127, Fall 2010 © Wiley Periodicals, Inc., and the American Evaluation Association. Published online in Wiley Online Library (wileyonlinelibrary.com) • DOI: 10.1002/ev.340

Yet in neither of these cases is there a genuine understanding of what a critical evaluation might be.

Because critique is in the language of theory, and because this discourse often takes some work to penetrate, our explanations of critical approaches to those outside the academy are often met with glazed eyes. Our approach in this chapter is to offer one example of how theory can be useful in an evaluation context. The critical approach we use is critical race theory (CRT). Parker (2004) proposed that CRT could be of use in evaluation, but to our knowledge there are no examples of this. This article seeks to correct this. Specifically, we use some key concepts from CRT to frame a series of evaluative studies of a school reform initiative. A variant of critical theory, CRT examines the individual, institutional, and cultural aspects of society that sustain oppressive structures. However, unlike critical theory, CRT is characterized by its insistence on placing race at the center of the analysis, and thus focusing on racial minorities and their relative subordination in a post–civil rights American culture (Crenshaw, Gotanda, Peller, & Thomas, 1995; Delgado & Stefancic, 2000).

We wish to be clear that, during the studies discussed below, we did not use the language of CRT for several reasons, including the fact that the funders wanted assessments of effectiveness. They were essentially looking for an instrumentalist critique—not what we understand as critique at all. However, as evaluators, it was clear to us that the school reform in question, James Comer's School Development Program (SDP) was being pressed to fit a mold not of its making, and this press was fundamentally about making the SDP consistent with White school reform. In essence, the evaluation funder was using us as a force toward making Comer's program a part of the majoritarian story of school reform. We will explain what we mean by this as we continue. The point for now is that we used our license as evaluators to instead "write against" that story. In CRT terms, we used the evaluation to construct a counternarrative.

In what follows, we will discuss critical race theory, the majoritarian story of school reform, and Comer's School Development Program. These sections will explain how we came to understand this evaluation context as fully "raced" and how CRT gave us tropes that guided our studies and our reporting. We then describe the evaluations that we conducted and how we wrote against dominant notions of school reform. Although we were unable to escape being the agents of the majoritarian story fully, we did work to make power flow back against that story. Indeed, this is one of the many lessons of CRT. Critique alone does not emancipate racialized others. Rather, it acknowledges racial hierarchy and shows how this affects the interpretation of reality.

Critical Race Theory

Critical theory is an attempt to expose and understand "inequalities and injustices in everyday social relationships" and to work "against oppression and for empowerment" (Freeman & Vasconcelos, this issue), and critical race theory is as an extension and/or application of critical theory. The inception of CRT dates back some 30 years to its origins in the critical legal studies (CLS) movement (Crenshaw et al., 1995). In legal studies, critical theory manifests itself as a critique of how legal consciousness and jurisprudence functioned to legitimate social power. However, by the early 80s, several legal scholars of color had become dissatisfied with CLS, arguing that despite its critical lenses, it did not adequately address issues of race and racial oppression in debates about the law, the legal system and American society. Seeking a new discourse that not only included race, but also placed it directly at the center of analysis, they conceptualized critical race theory.

Over the past 15 years, CRT has been taken up by scholars in different disciplines, including education. Solorzano and Yosso (2001) argue that a critical race analysis of educational contexts "challenges the dominant discourse of race and racism as they relate to education by examining how educational theories, policies, and practices are used to subordinate certain racial and ethnic groups" (p. 472). Further, like critical theory, the ultimate goal of CRT is to work toward "the elimination of racism as part of a larger goal of eliminating other forms of subordination" (p. 472). Critical race theory in education is shaped by five major tenets: (a) centrality of race and racism and their intersectionality with other forms of subordination, (b) challenge to dominant ideology, (c) commitment to social justice, (d) centrality of experiential knowledge, and (e) a transdisciplinary perspective (p. 473).

For our purposes, we take up two popular concepts associated with critical race theory: interest convergence and whiteness as property. The notion of interest convergence, first coined by critical race legal theorist Derrick Bell, argues that significant change in the social circumstances of people of color (i.e., racial equality) will only come about if and when such change is also in the interest of Whites. As applied here, we argue that the Comer program (which was originally targeted toward predominantly Black schools) would have to fit a majoritarian (White) model of school reform in order to obtain the approval of those in power. Put differently, the program would have to serve the interest of the majority if it wanted to move its agenda forward.

Furthermore, the program's ability to stake its claim as a successful school reform model hinged directly on its ability to prove its effectiveness. We argue that, from a CRT perspective, *effectiveness* can be understood as a representational form of whiteness. As Harris (1995) noted, privilege and other benefits have long been associated with whiteness. As such, whiteness has become a valuable asset to possess and thus can be viewed as a form of property. In the majoritarian story of school reform, the criteria for effectiveness are steeped in White ways of assessing and valuing the world. Consequently, like whiteness, the definition of *effectiveness* is carefully monitored so that only certain programs meeting stringent criteria can reap the benefit of its value. In the White school reform model, achievement was the primary criteria and this was to be enforced by higher standards and accountability. School reform initiatives then were to be judged by how well schools met these imposed achievement standards.

As the evaluators for the Comer School Development Program, we understood that we were being asked to uphold and sustain the majoritarian story by demonstrating the program's effectiveness as validated by means and measures traditionally associated with White school reform. Moreover, we would later be called upon to extend our roles as facilitators of interest convergence by demonstrating that the educational benefits the Comer program had brought to the predominantly Black, urban schools were also in the interest of White, rural schools. Ironically, a form of color blindness, which is roundly critiqued within CRT, turned out to be necessary for this interest convergence.

White School Reform

There have been many waves of school reform in the history of public education in the United States. The most recent one began in 1983 with the publication of A Nation at Risk (National Commission of Excellence in Education [NCEE], 1983). This manifesto was prepared under the auspices of the Reagan administration and began with the claim that public education was characterized by a "rising tide of mediocrity" (p. 1). This manifesto set the stage for a new federal presence in education that was to establish excellence as the goal. What was left unsaid in this publication is as important as what was said. Excellence was to displace equity, which was seen as the cause of mediocrity. That is to say, school reform was a backlash against school desegregation.

White school reform was more than a backlash though. It was a radical reassertion that public education was to serve the economy (Noblit & Philipsen, 1993). In the early 1980s, the United States was losing its share of the global market to other countries, especially Japan and Germany, and U.S. business leaders blamed the education system for this lack of competitiveness. White school reform was then to generate the talent the economy needed—thus the focus on excellence. There were a host of school reform efforts sponsored under White school reform. These efforts were seen as designs in which schools would be held accountable for higher standards of achievement through making schools and schooling more systemic. Schools were to become more "tightly coupled" (Meyer & Rowan, 1978). This era was also marked by a lack of faith in public institutions and a belief that taxes were too high in the United States—also undercutting international competition. Thus White school reform was to be accomplished with little or no additional resources given to schools. White school reform was about a better-engineered educational system. Schools were not sufficiently instrumental in their operations and especially in producing student achievement. By becoming more instrumental, money could be saved while enhancing the competitiveness of business internationally.

The Counternarrative

James Comer's School Development Program was already in existence when the White school reform era began. Comer had begun working in inner-city, segregated schools in New Haven, Connecticut, during the late 1960s. As an African American, Comer's emphasis was on empowering Black schools and communities to serve all of the developmental needs of their children. This child-development focus included much more than academics and asked schools how they could develop the whole child. After several years, the Comer model came to incorporate three mechanisms: the school planning and management team, the parent team, and the student and staff support team. These teams were to guide the decision making for school-level efforts and ensure broad participation in decision making. The Comer model also had three principles: consensus, collaboration, and no fault. Consensus was to discourage voting and a winning–losing logic in decision making. Everyone was to work toward efforts acceptable to everyone. Collaboration meant having everyone (parents, educators, and students) involved in the process. No-fault decision making was to discourage the assignment of blame and move directly toward shared responsibility for better education and development of the children.

The mechanisms and principles clearly are not race based. Yet Comer's School Development Program was focused on schools that served students of color. Moreover, the schools themselves saw the SDP as a program run by people of color for people of color. The mechanisms themselves had faith that people of color were fully able to fashion the types of changes needed in their schools. The SDP provided training on the process, and these sessions were often facilitated by Comer staff of color working with parents and educators of color to prepare to implement the SDP in their schools. James Comer's School Development Program became the only Black school reform initiative during the White school reform era. This meant Comer had to work against as well as with the larger logic of White school reform.

Our counternarrative to the majoritarian story of White school reform was constructed over several years. Although the final book about the work was published in 2008 (Malloy, Malloy, & Noblit, 2008), we were engaged in evaluation and research activities with Comer from 1997 to 2004. The work was funded through three grants, two from the Rockefeller Foundation and one from the federal government. In each case, funding was tied to both short-term evaluation efforts, such as evaluating specific training processes, and long-term studies of effectiveness. Each project was enmeshed in White school reform, in that the funding was viewed as a way for Comer to demonstrate that it was an effective school reform and thus worthy of continued funding from private foundations and the federal government. Our evaluation work became part of this ongoing struggle.

Evaluating Comer

Evaluation Study I

Seeking outside evaluators to investigate the success of the Comer model, the Rockefeller Foundation selected our UNC-CH team through a limited but competitive process. Our biracial research team was multidisciplinary (sociology, administration, and curriculum) and had a record of doing studies of race and education as well as school reform. We, the Comer staff, and the Foundation came together to determine whether, and how, the study could go forward. In some sense, Comer had no leverage here—he had to accept the study, and our team, in order to continue to be sponsored by the Foundation.

The purpose of the study was to identify successful Comer schools and explore the factors that contributed to their success. We selected schools that were effective on a range of measures, from achievement to parent involvement. The SDP identified 37 candidates and, after careful scrutiny, we selected 11. Five of the 11 sites were targeted for in-depth case studies. The methodology selected was a comparative case design involving three on-site visits in each of the schools over the period of a year.

Naming the study "The Comer Success Study" signaled our walking away from the prominent presumption in the White school reform literature that a reform design without major curricular elements could be effective. Moreover, it also sharpened our study design. The Rockefeller Foundation was interested in some determination as to whether Comer schools were effective generally. We felt this question had inherent problems in that no other reform at that time could make a similar claim based on an independent investigation. Thus if we had taken on the general effectiveness question, Comer would have been the only reform held to that standard, reinforcing the perception that Black school reform efforts need interrogation where others do not.

In our evaluation, we documented how the elements of the program interacted with local contexts to create (and/or not) success in achievement, parent involvement, and discipline. In the end, we generated evidence that there were successful Comer schools and determined that they could attribute these successes to the Comer reform initiative. Although there are many lessons learned (see Noblit, Malloy, & Malloy, 2001), we argued that Comer's emphasis on planning management and widespread participation allowed these schools to "take charge of change" (p. 114). We ended our analysis by directly addressing how the Comer story countered conventional wisdom—although we did not directly use the language of critical race theory.

NEW DIRECTIONS FOR EVALUATION • DOI: 10.1002/ev

We discussed the "tacit assumptions about schooling" and "bureaucratic assumptions about structuring schools" (pp. 132–134) and then responded with "counter-assumptions for structuring schools" (pp. 134–135). The book ended by comparing what we had learned to an article that we thought summarized White school reform's lessons. In so doing we embraced the CRT principle of interest convergence, and showed how the Comer approach demonstrates the principle with the exception of the focus on curricula and instruction. Instead, the SDP's focus on child development was noted as an alternative.

We had obviously taken sides in this study and in doing so were able to assist the SDP in gaining a form of property—the claim of effectiveness. In doing so, we also named the key trope of White school reform—the necessity for curricula and instruction emphases—and challenged its necessity for a Black school reform initiative. Comer promoted the book we wrote as a way for schools to talk with their district administrations and school boards about what the SDP was able to accomplish. The book became a claim to legitimation for a Black school reform model in the face of the dominant narrative of White school reform.

Evaluation Study II

The Rockefeller Foundation saw "The Comer Success Study" as establishing that the SDP was an effective school reform model. In short, the Foundation found our counternarrative sufficiently compelling to fund a second study examining systemic reform—where school districts were the primary locus of SDP efforts rather than individual schools. Here, our efforts were geared toward examining what was needed for a school reform effort to be effective on a district level. We conducted case studies of four large school districts. In systemic reform, the majoritarian story was situated in a set of assumptions about alignment within and across the levels (district, school, classroom), and between key processes (curricula, instruction, assessment, professional development, etc.).

Here again was a rather instrumental story line, and one that the SDP addressed in its inimical way. The Comer process emphasized inclusion of a wide set of participants and trusted them to decide what was the best way to improve the education of young people. Where the majoritarian story focused on test outcomes, the SDP countered with a focus on a fuller model of child development. Where White school reform was about tightening the linkages and reducing variability of local efforts, our case studies revealed that systemic reform through the SDP worked through a similar process across districts and schools, but that district and school efforts that were rather different could still be effective in serving children and raising test scores.

Again our counternarrative demonstrated that property was a key theme. However, the key difference here was in the ownership. When schools and districts designed their own reform efforts, they owned them in powerful ways. In these large urban districts, the racial identity of the SDP as a Black reform effort was empowering as well. That is to say, although there was "interest convergence" between White school reform's emphasis on accountability and the outcomes produced by Comer schools and districts, it was clear to these majority–minority cities that systemic reform via the SDP was more community based. It invited people of color to the table and gave them a voice and a role in establishing a consensus on what was best for the full development of their children. Because local efforts were tailored to the district, school, and communities served, it was evident that the stakeholders' ideas and values were being used to reform the schools and districts in ways the communities valued. Our report and subsequent book demonstrated that the SDP not only had legs as a whole school reform effort, but as a systemic reform initiative as well (Malloy et al., 2008).

Evaluation Study III

Following these studies, the SDP itself contracted with us to evaluate aspects of their efforts. We studied their professional development efforts, their data systems, new curricula and instructional initiatives, and their expansion into rural schools and districts. These efforts were funded through federal grants and had two purposes. First, our evaluations demonstrated to the funders that the SDP was engaged in continual improvement, a key trope of White school reform. Second, our evaluations helped the Comer staff better understand how they were different from, and sometimes similar to, White school reform designs. The new curricula and instruction initiatives were responses to schools and districts feeling the press to have such programs but simultaneously not wishing to buy a packaged reform, such as Success for All, which largely scripts instruction (McKinney & Noblit, 2005). Our evaluation studies helped the SDP stay as true as possible to its commitments to local goal setting and implementation, and respond to the needs of their stakeholders.

The expansion of the SDP into rural districts tested its identity as Black reform. The rural districts now adopting the model were more diverse than the urban districts we had studied in that they had sizeable White student populations. Consequently, the SDP faced a dilemma. As a Black school reform effort, they were committed to working for minority student populations. However, these new districts had a lower-class White population with significant child development needs. This led Comer to focus more on poverty, and they adopted the work of Ruby Payne to facilitate the transition. The evaluation team found this last move problematic. Payne's approach is essentially a deficit model, thus playing into existing race and class prejudices. Instead, we favored CRT's concept of intersectionality (Crenshaw, 1995), where race and class (and gender and sexual orientation) were seen as different, but sharing points of intersectionality. Unfortunately, the SDP was facing this dilemma at a time when CRT's understanding of intersectionality was rather fledgling and had yet to be translated into education.

NEW DIRECTIONS FOR EVALUATION • DOI: 10.1002/ev

Our collaboration with the SDP came to an end, as so many evaluative efforts do. School reform efforts were facing decreased funding as policy makers decided that they were too expensive to sustain. The shift to the politics of accountability discussed earlier put the emphasis on testing and left the means to achieve higher test scores up to districts and schools (and also left the means largely unfunded). The SDP, like so many other school reform efforts, now had to rely on local funding to sustain itself, and the large-scale evaluation we had been pursuing was simply too expensive to sustain. This denouement is instructive, as we will discuss below.

Learning From Countering

There are several lessons we learned from framing evaluation as critical race theory. First, as is obvious to all evaluators, our hierarchically-organized society tends to deploy evaluation onto those lower in the hierarchy. This is why evaluators have worked hard to develop collaborative (O'Sullivan, 2004) and participative (Cousins & Earl, 1995) forms of evaluation. Our experience with CRT suggests that these approaches, for all their good points, are ameliorative. With CRT the intent is to speak back to power— to counter the majoritarian White story. Thus, there is clearly some risk to this approach. We minimized the risk by not naming CRT and by speaking directly to the interests of funders and policy makers. In doing so, we were able to articulate how the SDP achieved more than the narrow achievement goal, even though local efforts took on a variety of forms. This in part legitimated the SDP but did not change the majoritarian story. We ended up negotiating an exception to the rule rather than a change in the rule. Nevertheless, if we had failed in our articulation of the counternarrative both our funding and the future of the SDP could have been jeopardized.

Second, and relatedly, a CRT approach is not likely to become a common evaluative strategy. It is designed primarily to speak about the central ity of race. Although we would argue that every aspect of American life is marked by race, it is clearly true that not all share this view and even if they do they may feel this assertion itself creates too much controversy. Thus we believe CRT will likely be limited to evaluation of programs that are racially marked in rather definitive ways. For such evaluations, the evaluation team also needs to be sufficiently knowledgeable of both CRT and of the majoritarian story at play to articulate the counterstory and its implications. In our own experience, this is not always the case. We often evaluate programs for which we have minimal background knowledge, at least initially. Though we learn much as we proceed, we still think CRT requires a considerable knowledge base from the beginning. This, and the requirement that race be centered, means that CRT will not become a popular form of evaluation. There are culturally responsive evaluation designs (Hood, Hopson, & Frierson, 2005; SenGupta, Hopson, & Thompson-Robinson, 2004) that may be viable alternatives when CRT seems too confrontational.

Third, many evaluations are driven to explain ends or outcomes. Even process evaluations are about the linkages between things. In these cases, our use of language is explanatory. We explain how things work. Evaluations utilizing CRT are no exception to this. However, they also use language to try to change a discourse. We do this by articulating the dominant story line in the wider discourse and by articulating its counterstory. In doing so, we discern which CRT themes are better for critiquing the dominant story. In the evaluations discussed here we used interest convergence and whiteness as property, and we believe that they assisted us in countering White school reform. In this articulation out from program to wider discourse there are similarities with other critical approaches.

Nevertheless, there may have been other themes that should have been developed. For instance, we might have opted to talk about the inability of White school reform to recognize, as effective, programs that lacked a curricula and instructional emphasis in terms of the differend. According to Duncan (2006), the *differend*, a notion attributed to French philosopher Jean-François Lyotard that has recently been taken up by critical race theorists, occurs when a concept or term (such as *effectiveness*) acquires conflicting meaning for two parties. The party that suffers the differend, in this case the SDP, is forced to try to articulate their reality in the language of the dominant party (White school reform), and thus SDP's truth is not accorded full respect, nor value, on its own terms.

Finally, our success in using CRT with the SDP ended up being time and epoch limited. The school reform era is over. The powerful have the prerogative to change their story line when and how they wish. Recall that school reform was first initiated to improve school outcomes at no or little additional cost. Yet the school reform era demonstrated that improvement would take significant, ongoing, additional funds. This, and the level of complexity uncovered in reform evaluations and studies, led policy makers to abandon school reform and to embrace accountability rather solely. Thus our CRT counterstory may have addressed an existing majoritarian story, but it did not lessen the power of White policy makers to change the story when they wished. Whether CRT could be used to do so, we are not sure—but we will be thinking this through in our future work. It is one thing to counter a story. It is another to shape the future story lines of the powerful.

In conclusion, CRT is a member of the family of critical approaches. It differs from some other critical approaches in that its focus on race and countering dominant narratives leads it to speak directly to and against power. Although it is pessimistic about emancipation (as it requires Whites to give up their power), it accepts the goal of enlightenment both for the race dominated and the race dominating. Although our experience with it has been productive, CRT should be used only when race is acknowledged to be central, when the evaluators are quite knowledgeable of the wider discourses on race and critical theories, and when the evaluand can be articulated against a dominant story line.

References

Cousins, J. B., & Earl, L. M. (Eds.). (1995). *Participatory evaluation in education: Studies of evaluation use and organizational learning.* New York: Routledge.

Crenshaw, K., Gotanda, N., Peller, G., & Thomas, K. (Eds.). (1995). *Critical race theory: The key writings that formed the movement.* New York: The New Press.

Crenshaw, K. W. (1995). Mapping the margins: Intersectionality, identity politics, and violence against women of color. In K. Crenshaw, N. Gotanda, G. Peller, & K. Thomas (Eds.), *Critical race theory: The key writings that formed the movement* (pp. 357–383). New York: The New Press.

Delgado, R., & Stefancic, J. (Eds.). (2000). *Critical race theory: The cutting edge.* Philadelphia: Temple University Press.

Duncan, G. (2006). Critical race ethnography in education: Narrative, inequality, and the problem of epistemology. In A. Dixson & C. Rousseau (Eds.), *Critical race theory in education: All God's children got a song* (pp. 191–212). New York: Routledge.

Harris, C. I. (1995). Whiteness as property. In K. Crenshaw, N. Gotanda, G. Peller, & K. Thomas (Eds.), *Critical race theory: The key writings that formed the movement* (pp. 276–291). New York: The New Press.

Hood, S., Hopson, R. K., & Frierson, H. (2005). *The role of culture and cultural context: A mandate for inclusion, the discovery of truth, and understanding in evaluative theory and practice.* Greenwich, CT: Information Age Publishing.

Malloy, W., Malloy, C., & Noblit, G. (2008). *Bringing systemic reform to life: School district reform and Comer schools.* Cresskill, NJ: Hampton Press.

McKinney, M., & Noblit, G. (2005). Success for all. In W. Pink and G. Noblit (Eds.), *Cultural matters: Lessons learned from field studies from several leading school reform strategies* (pp. 1–34). Cresskill, NJ: Hampton Press.

Meyer, J. W., & Rowan, B. (1978). The structure of educational organizations. In M. W. Meyer et al. (Eds.), *Environments and organizations.* San Francisco: Jossey-Bass.

National Commission of Excellence in Education (NCEE). (1983). *A nation at risk: The imperative for educational reform.* Washington, DC: U.S. Government Printing Office.

Noblit, G., & Philipsen, M. (1993). Tricky business. *The High School Journal, 76*(4), 260–272.

Noblit, G. W , Malloy, C. E., & Malloy, W. (Eds.). (2001). *The kids got smarter: Case studies of successful Comer schools.* Cresskill, NJ: Hampton Press.

O'Sullivan, R. (2004). *Practicing evaluation: A collaborative approach.* Thousand Oaks, CA: Sage.

Parker, L. (2004). Commentary: Can critical theories of or on race be used in evaluation research in education? In V. Thomas & F. Stevens (Eds.), *Co-constructing a responsive evaluation framework. New Directions for Evaluation, 101,* 85–93.

SenGupta, S., Hopson, R., & Thompson-Robinson, M. (2004). Cultural competence in evaluation: An overview. In M. Thompson-Robinson, R. Hopson, & S. SenGupta (Eds.), *In search of cultural competence in evaluation: Toward principles and practices. New Directions for Evaluation, 102,* 5–19.

Solorzano, D. G., & Yosso, T. J. (2001). Critical race and Latcrit theory and method: Counter-storytelling. *Qualitative Studies in Education, 14*(4), 471–495.

GEORGE W. NOBLIT is the Joseph R. Neikirk Distinguished Professor of Sociology of Education and in the School of Education at the University of North Carolina at Chapel Hill. His work includes extensive evaluation and research studies of Comer schools and the A+ Schools Program, an arts-based school reform program.

MICHELLE JAY is an assistant professor of Social Foundations in the Department of Educational Studies at the University of South Carolina. Her research interests include critical race theory in education, the use of qualitative methodology in educational research and evaluation, and culturally responsive evaluation practices.

NEW DIRECTIONS FOR EVALUATION • DOI: 10.1002/ev

Mabry, L. (2010). Critical social theory evaluation: Slaying the dragon. In M. Freeman (Ed.), *Critical social theory and evaluation practice. New Directions for Evaluation, 127*, 83–98.

7

Critical Social Theory Evaluation: Slaying the Dragon

Linda Mabry

Abstract

Values underlie evaluations, but there is no consensus as to whose values should found evaluators' judgments of program quality. The controversial position of critical social theory evaluators—that societal values trump those of evaluation commissioners—is explored in terms of professional issues and standards, historical evolutions, philosophical trajectories, and social responsibility. Attention is given to risks, compensations, and opportunity costs associated with taking (or not) a critical social theory approach to evaluation. © Wiley Periodicals, Inc., and the American Evaluation Association.

Values are at the etymological heart of evaluation. Program evaluators try to determine the value of programs: *valuable enough to preserve rather than terminate? valuable enough to invest in improvements?* Establishing the value of social and educational programs raises complex questions at the furthest end of the taxonomy of cognitive objectives (Bloom, Englehart, Furst, Hill, & Krathwohl, 1956). Such questions, evaluators would all agree, require critical thinking and careful judgment. More complicated than the cognitive issues are the social issues that add human diversity and impact to the process of evaluating program merit and shortcoming: *valuable to whom? valuable according to which (whose) criteria?* Evaluators find little agreement among themselves about the appropriate role of diverse social values in determining the value of a program or the nature, criteria, or indicators of program quality. Those who promote attention to the values of stakeholders beyond those of program managers or funders, the key or "primary intended users" (Patton, 1997), often refer optimistically to the importance of building consensus. But the diversity of stakeholder interests may be irreconcilable, and evaluation's capacity to clarify differences may cement dissensus. Moreover, for federally funded programs, the concepts of need-to-know and right-to-know audiences imply that every taxpayer, every citizen, every resident is a remote stakeholder, introducing a diversity of social values that could overwhelm an evaluation.

As if the cognitive and social aspects were insufficiently challenging, consensus within the profession is even rarer regarding the appropriate and actual role of the evaluator's own values in evaluating a program. At one end of the spectrum are evaluators who favor what might be called "technical" practice. These practitioners tend to equate subjectivity and personal values with bias, tend to worry about consequent threats to validity, tend to endorse de-emphasis of personal values, and to seek objectivity. At other points on the spectrum are evaluators who take subjective judgment as fundamental in determining the value of a program, who see the interpretation of program quality as naturally value laden. These practitioners accept the role of an evaluator's personal values in the process of evaluation and may work to offset their own with the multiple perspectives of stakeholders and with competing notions of value.

Stakeholder and personal values thread through the valuing—the evaluating—of a social program. A dozen or more approaches to evaluation, the number dependent on the classification scheme (see, e.g., Shadish, Cook, & Leviton, 1991; Stufflebeam, 2001; Stufflebeam, Madaus, & Kellaghan, 2000), manifest different degrees to which evaluators consciously accept stakeholder and personal values as part of the challenge. These differences are not resolved in the standards and principles formulated by professional evaluation organizations (American Evaluation Association, 1995; Joint Committee on Standards for Educational Evaluation, 1994). Rather, the swirl of approaches has obstructed the development of certification procedures or the enforcement of a code of conduct to guide competent and ethical practice (King, Stevahn, Ghere, & Minnema, 2001; Kirkhart, 1981; Mabry, in press).

As medieval maps warned, beyond this point, there be dragons. However, from ideological points beyond comes the issue taken up in this volume: What is the evaluator's role in promoting social values that may conflict with those of clients and other stakeholders? For about two decades, evaluation approaches that champion social participation, values, and justice have been controversial (Stufflebeam, 1994; Stufflebeam et al., 2001). The authors of this issue urge and describe *critical social theory evaluation* as a practice that undertakes social critique and proactive social reform:

NEW DIRECTIONS FOR EVALUATION • DOI: 10.1002/ev

. . . we are arguing for taking the side of social justice, and what that means and involves is part of what the inquiry process must both determine and then use as the basis for action. (Freeman & Vasconcelos, this issue, pp. 10–11)

[Evaluators] are not only about making value judgments of the existing education system, but are also steering future educational systems. (Segerholm, this issue, p. 67)

. . . a critical orientation for evaluation is necessarily self-reflexive of its own practice and how that practice serves to empower or disempower . . . Our biggest failure [in our evaluation] was not directly addressing the issue of power and how power . . . halted deliberation of key issues. (Freeman, Preissle, & Havick, this issue, pp. 46 and 53)

. . . reflection revealed that the evaluation was ultimately both consistent and inconsistent with the beliefs of a critical evaluator. . . and also had elements that may have inadvertently sustained the power relationships we sought to equalize. (Hooper, this issue, p. 22)

[Evaluators should] not reinforce negative conceptions of young people . . . [but] the current use of evaluation in the field of youth development serves to maintain status quo for young people. (Zeller-Berkman, this issue, p. 42)

. . . we used the evaluation to construct a counternarrative. . . Although we were unable to escape being the agents of the majoritarian story fully, we did work to make power flow back against that story. (Noblit & Jay, this issue, p. 72)

If social reform is the dragon to be found in these environs, perhaps the creature has breathed into evaluation a fiery new life that tempers evaluators, burning with social responsibility, for daunting challenges. But some will surely consider such evaluators slain by the dragon and resurrected as political activists.

Some distinctions are needed. This text represents an attempt to clarify how evaluation as a professional field has reached the point of critical social theory evaluation; then, looking back historically, to distinguish critical social theory evaluation from its predecessors and current competitors and, looking forward philosophically, to distinguish a critical social theory concept from a postmodern concept of evaluation.

Historical Development

Critical theory is also called *radicalism* and, in Britain, *cultural studies*. Critical theory refers less to theory than to the examination and critique of society. It is part of the history of the search for knowledge and, with enriched understanding, the improvement of the human condition. This quest to understand has advanced from superstition to mythology to religion, to science and to social science. In social science, the quest began with a focus borrowed from the physical sciences, a positivist search for the real (Compte, 1851; Mill, 1863/1891). Partly as a reaction to confidence in objective reality and partly in response to its own conceptual impulses, an interpretivist, hermeneutic method emerged (see Cronbach, 1975; Guba, 1990).

In the West, social science originated in ideas about society formulated during the fourth through sixth centuries BCE by Socrates, Plato, and Aristotle. Lost in Western Europe during the Dark Ages but rediscovered during the Age of Enlightenment, Greek notions about government developed into the idea that the social contract could be studied and improved (Rousseau, 1755/1992). A century later, the most famous critical theorist, Karl Marx, developed a critique of capitalist society (Marx & Engels, 1867/1996). Shortly before World War II, Marx's work influenced the creation of the Frankfurt School (Adorno, 1978; Habermas, 1987), which undertook systematic examination of the role of societal values and institutions in creating and sustaining political and economic ideologies and inequalities. In our own times, critical theory has been invigorated by feminist (see Bleier, 1986; Lather, 1991; Mauthner, Birch, Jessop, & Miller, 2002; Sutton, 1998) and race-based perspectives (see Banks, 2006; Ogbu, 1978).

In comparison to the direct infusion of critical theory into social science, postmodernism sidled in from art, literary criticism, and philosophy. The term arose in the context of paintings that were no longer representations of visible reality but, rather, allusionary portrayals of ineffable meanings, compositions considered to be beyond the modern. French poststructuralists, taking literary criticism toward philosophy, focused on "deconstructing" the unseen presence of the author in the text (Derrida, 1976), on revealing personal perspectives the author had disguised as facts. They objected to "metanarratives," textual accounts that extolled social progress that benefited the powerful at the expense of the vulnerable, those who were simultaneously subjected and objectified as mere cogs in the social wheel (Foucault, 1973, 1980). Thus, postmodernists surfaced the crisis of representation (Lyotard, 1979/1984; see also M. Greene, 1994) and, questioning the authority of the author to represent the perspectives and experiences of others, the crisis of legitimation (Habermas, 1975). They deplored technology's capacity to proliferate projections of the real that obscured what was actually real (Baudrillard, 1983) and thereby to facilitate manipulation of human consciousness and of the masses.

Postmodernists focused on power, its implications for individuals and for society, its acquisition and institutionalization, the mechanisms by which the few dominate the many, the co-opting and preoccupying of the victims. Pursuing these ideas to their logical conclusion, postmodernists reached the point of realizing that empowering the oppressed would transform them into oppressors. Thus, any action taken within the social system, however innocent or well-intended, would either contribute to the oppressive status quo or to its replacement by yet another oppressive social system.

What's a social scientist to do? Two practical options surfaced from the philosophical mire. *Extreme postmodernists* (Rosenau, 1992) retreat. They take the position that postmodernism in social science entails refusal to conduct studies that will be misused by oppressors, refusal to contribute to a system that selects what will be considered knowledge, refusal to play the game or to be played by its historic winners. Retreating instead into private realms might take the form of condemning the world—recall Jean-Paul Sartre's existentialist denunciation, "Hell is other people" (1944)—or retreat might take the form of laughing at the world, carnival. No one is immune. Not only postmodernists but virtually everyone experiences distrust of authority and of social institutions, disillusionment, and cynicism. That is, postmodernism in the extreme sense may be understood not just as a philosophical framework or as a practical choice, but as a social condition, whether or not it is recognized by those who experience it.

Affirmative postmodernists (Rosenau, 1992), on the other hand, backtrack to critical theory, bringing with them a humility and self-reflectiveness suggested by the postmodern insight. For them, the oppression of the poor and disenfranchised is all too real, not merely philosophical, and retreat would be socially and personally irresponsible (Mabry, 1997). In the affirmative sense, postmodernism in social science may be understood as a relentless effort to reveal hegemony. It focuses methodology on the amelioration of oppression through the focused collection and analysis of data and through strategic dissemination of results. At least so far, postmodernism appears to be the end of the line in social science philosophy.

Critical Theory and Evaluation

Paralleling social science to some degree, evaluation has evolved on its own time line, while basically continuing to subscribe to the so-called "modernist project" of improving society through knowledge. Because programs are conceived and implemented to improve aspects of society, evaluations commissioned to understand their effects and their effectiveness contribute to that project.

Spurred in modern times by U.S. desire to win the space race of the 1950s, federally funded programs to improve public education included requirements that the programs be evaluated to determine which were most productive. Early evaluations focused on goal achievement (e.g., Scriven, 1972), managerial decision making (e.g., Stufflebeam, 1987), cost–benefit analyses, and the measuring of program objectives and impact (see Christie & Alkin, 2005). Under complaints about overemphasis on statistical information in lieu of site-based data collection, educational evaluations gradually began to give more attention to program stakeholders—their experiences and perspectives (Guba, 1978; Guba & Lincoln, 1989), and their utilization

Figure 7.1. Evolution of Evaluation Approaches From a Critical Theory Perspective

Technical: Managerial and outcomes-oriented evaluation, impact evaluation, cost-benefits analyses, reliance on quantitative indicator systems

Interpretivist: Contextualized, qualitative evaluation with attention to multiple perspectives and conditionalities affecting program outcomes

Stakeholder-oriented: Evaluation attending to the perspectives and experiences of stakeholders, with increasing awareness of the need for culturally sensitive methods

Participatory: Evaluation sharing responsibility with stakeholders, sometimes with the goal of restructuring social and personnel hierarchies

Ideologically oriented: Evaluation promoting explicit values (e.g., democracy) and aiming at such critical theory goals as social reform and social justice

Postmodern:
(a) *Extreme postmodernist*–Retreat away from evaluation because evaluations are commissioned and used by the powerful to sustain oppression and because attempts to redress inequalities are ultimately futile
(b) *Affirmative postmodernist*–Return to critical social theory evaluation with an understanding of the need for self-critical practice alert to the possibilities that evaluation itself could entrench oppression

of evaluation results (Patton, 1997). Later, stakeholder participation (J.C. Greene, 1997, 2006; Mertens, 2005) and empowerment (Fetterman, 1996) became goals for some evaluators. Later still, use of evaluation to promote social justice and explicit ideologies, especially democracy (House, 1993; House & Howe, 1999), moved evaluation into the realm of critical theory. (See Figure 7.1.)

In this chronology, no phase achieved consensus or avoided controversy (e.g., Stufflebeam, 1994; Stufflebeam et al., 2001). Emerging approaches found adherents but also engendered ongoing resistance. From the point of view of critical theory, evaluators began to construe their responsibilities as more than technical, more than providing information to benefit society by facilitating data-driven decision making. They inched toward a more explicitly value-laden perspective and toward practice designed to promote specific ideologies or societal redress (see Mabry, in press).

Thus, one strand of evaluation moved toward critical social theory evaluation (Freeman & Vasconcelos, this issue), evaluation in the service of fairness, and the redistribution of power and wealth. This approach invites question and challenge. In addition to being subject to the charge that its goals differ from or exceed those of evaluation, critical social theory evaluation is also fair game for deconstructionist wariness regarding the author behind the evaluation text: *whose idea of fairness is this?* A postmodernist perspective would consider whether an explicitly ideological stance might amount to an assumption of undeserved authority, for example, assuming the authority to define fairness and to use a stipulated definition to dominate others: *who benefits from this definition and its implications, and who suffers?*

So, challenges from two directions that critical social theory evaluation is too little about evaluation and too much about social restructuring should be expected. For evaluators taking a technical view, the problem is that critical social theory evaluation abandons the basic purposes and goals of evaluation in favor of political instigation. For extreme postmodernists, the problem is that attempts to reform society are futile, that success would merely place the crowns on other heads. On the other hand, critical social theory evaluation is itself a challenge to traditional evaluators' psychologically and politically too-comfortable role as finders and deliverers of truth with no further obligation. For critical social theory evaluators, both traditional avoidance of social issues and postmodern refusal to engage are socially and ethically irresponsible.

Critical Social Theory Evaluation and the Standards

Evaluation may be usefully studied from the standpoint of the critical theory challenge and, reciprocally, critical social theory evaluation may be examined from the perspective of long-standing codes of professional conduct such as Program Evaluation Standards (Joint Committee on Standards for Educational Evaluation, 1994). Intersection of the four categories of the Standards (accuracy, utility, propriety, and feasibility) with the aims of critical social theory evaluation surface thorny considerations.

Accuracy

The Standards themselves can be interpreted as a sign that evaluation has long operated on a modernist (and positivist or objectivist) assumption of truth and reality: that what is observable and measurable about programs is real, not solipsistic illusion, and that reliable evaluation data and valid findings are in one-to-one correspondence with the real. From this perspective, the evaluator's task is to apprehend the reality of the program and to represent it accordingly.

Even from a technical point of view, the Accuracy Standards present no small challenge: gaining comprehensive knowledge of a program, its intents and mechanisms and outcomes, its merits and shortcomings. Socially sensitive and critical perspectives hugely complicate the challenge by questioning not only whether accuracy has been achieved in a given instance, but also the nature of accuracy: *accurate in which contexts and under what conditions* (interpretivist), *accurate according to whom* (stakeholder-oriented)? *Who was part of the process of determining what is accurate* (participatory), and *how did their value commitments affect their judgments* (ideologically oriented)?

If what is true is a matter of perspective, and if perspective is conditioned by personal values, then accuracy is idiosyncratic to some degree. For most evaluators, this chain of logic and its conclusion are insufferable. Fortunately, just as relativism can be espoused without considering absolute

NEW DIRECTIONS FOR EVALUATION • DOI: 10.1002/ev

relativism inevitable, and just as all interpretations need not be accorded equal credibility, evaluation accuracy may be judged on such bases as comprehensiveness; the field testing, triangulation, validation, and peer review of data; the warranting and logic of findings. But even the most careful data collection and analysis cannot guarantee accuracy.

This more complicated view strips accuracy of binary meaning. An evaluation cannot be simply *accurate or not*, and the Accuracy Standards cannot be simply met or not. Rather, accuracy assumes the less satisfying characteristic of a continuum along which data, findings, and reports are *more or less accurate*. Determining the degree of accuracy of an evaluation is reduced to a judgment call. So, the Accuracy Standards are no fortress for objectivity, no sorcerer's charm against personal values or subjective bias.

Utility

Although evaluators might easily agree that evaluations should be useful for making program improvements, as the Utility Standards urge, there are long-standing disagreements about how much an evaluator should do to ensure productive and appropriate use of evaluation results. For some evaluators, assisting clients as they attempt to use feedback seems needed and responsible (e.g., Patton, 1997). To others, assistance after the fact transmogrifies evaluation into consulting (e.g., Scriven, 1998), dangerous because of the temptation to provide falsely positive findings in order to secure further employment.

From the standpoint of critical theory, utility involves more than helping clients improve program efficiency and functioning. It also requires the willingness to promote the interests of vulnerable and disempowered stakeholders (i.e., to speak truth to power), the willingness to consider the social implications of the uses to which an evaluation is likely to be put (i.e., to take a broad view of program effects and to plan for possible misuse), the willingness to risk discomfort and dismissal in actively seeking pro-social implementation of evaluation results (e.g., to be proactive in urging fairness). Even among evaluators sympathetic to critical theory, such willingness may be difficult to summon, varying with circumstances and individual integrity. Even for evaluators who see the need and summon the necessary strength, a troubling practical dilemma arises: *will pursuit of pro-social outcomes result in disregard rather than use of the evaluation? Will failure to pursue pro-social outcomes result in the evaluation's misuse?*

The intersection of the Utility Standards and postmodernism's awareness of the inevitability of hegemony brings another issue into focus: *should decision-makers favor the evaluator's values over those of program personnel and other stakeholders?* For a critical social theory evaluator, this issue demands introspection, a willingness to interrogate one's own conception of appropriate use of the evaluation. Theoretically at least, it is as possible for evaluators to misunderstand appropriate use as it is for clients to do so.

While the client can count on lived experience of the program to guide ideas about appropriate use, he or she is invested in the personal values reflected in the program; while an external evaluator can count on fresh eyes and systematically collected data, he or she is invested in the personal values reflected in the evaluation. There being no disinterested view, notions of appropriate use always involve someone's subjective values.

Another moat to cross: Individuals spend their lives gaining clarity about their own values, rarely if ever achieving perfect understanding of their values or how their emotions and values impact their judgment (Frijda, 1986; Ortony, Clore, & Collins, 1988). So, professional judgments as to what constitutes appropriate use of evaluation results are clouded not only by the personal values an evaluator might explicitly pursue but also by the implicit effects of hidden or dimly perceived values.

Propriety

The Standards consider propriety as a matter of compliance to the law, including conflicts of interest, and to ethical expectations, including due regard for the welfare of stakeholders and the disclosure of findings. For a critical social theory evaluator, propriety is also a matter of considering whether one has done the proper thing for society—for example, whether, because of an evaluation, social understandings deepened and become more humane, whether institutions begin to serve society better, whether equity is enhanced. But whether society has improved (or might improve) is yet another subjective judgment call. What one group will praise as progress another will decry as deterioration. So, whether an evaluation has (or might have) proper effects on society is subject to dispute.

Nor is it always clear that it is proper for the evaluator's judgment to override the intimate experience of program personnel and stakeholders. In a postmodern era in which authority is suspect, the evaluator cannot simply presume it appropriate for his or her conclusions or values to overrule those of decision-makers and other stakeholders. Errors of two types are possible. On one hand, clients might be well advised to exercise healthy skepticism in considering the work of a short-term outsider, one whose findings might point them toward unproductive territories. On the other hand, stakeholders pinched by evaluation results have been known to engage in blatant self-protection, to claim that interview data amount to "hearsay and innuendo" (Mabry, 1999; Mabry & Ettinger, 1999), to dismiss findings as "just one person's opinion" (Ernst-Slavit, personal communication, 2009), or to disregard findings entirely (Walker, 1997).

Feasibility

The Feasibility Standards advise evaluators to check the adequacy of resources for conducting an evaluation, to disrupt the program as little as possible, and to seek cooperation with stakeholders so as to gain access to data and to encourage appropriate use of results. To these admonishments, a critical theory outlook adds a demanding scope, the consideration of society writ large and writ small. Even in the abstract, such a broad scope calls into question the sufficiency of resources likely to be available for evaluation.

Moving from the abstract to practice raises a prior and perhaps more daunting feasibility obstacle: "[T]hose who seek our services as evaluators are put off by the notion of critical evaluation. . . . worried that the critique will be applied to them" (Noblit & Jay, this issue, p. 71). Negotiation of a critical theory approach to a particular evaluation seems highly unlikely, which suggests that critical social theory evaluation might be a covert practice in which evaluators conceal their values and the focus from clients. Perhaps an evaluator could rationalize secrecy by reference to a utilitarian ethic (Mill, 1863/1891) positing that casualties are acceptable in pursuit of the greater good and that the end justifies the means. But ethics, too, have evolved and have moved well beyond utilitarianism (see American Psychological Association, 2007; American Sociological Association, 1997; Kimmel, 1988; Mabry, 1999, 2008; Mauthner et al., 2002; Newman & Brown, 1996; Rawls, 1971). The shakiness of utilitarian grounds as an ethical justification for critical social theory evaluation would leave chinks in its armor.

So, the move to critical social theory evaluation, then on to postmodernism and back again, enormously complicates understanding and implementation of the Standards. The Standards themselves attempt more than just admonitions and proverbs by offering scenarios to illustrate situational implementation. But the need for scenarios to explain how to use the Standards is a virtual acknowledgment of the practical limitations of the Standards. In a given evaluation, adherence to one standard might complicate or undermine adherence to another, demanding prioritization (Mabry, 1999; see also House, 1995). Although the Standards do not encourage prioritization, critical social theory evaluation obviates the necessity of situational hierarchies based on evaluators' individual values. Negotiation of the Standards with an individual evaluator's beliefs and with the social issues raised by particular evaluations are both demanded.

Standards and standardization follow one logic, individuation another. Placing more trust in standards to promote competent, ethical practice means placing less trust in situational adaptations and individual valuing. Which works better for promoting professional competence? This question is important because of evaluation's intended (and actual) impact on program personnel and beneficiaries; it becomes grave when considering evaluation as a method for social engineering. To what extent are we willing to bet, not just the farm, but society on either a highly standardized or a highly personalized approach to evaluation? To what extent are we willing to bet on individual critical social theory evaluators' values for social restructuring?

Evaluation and Social Responsibility

Societies are constructed bit by bit from ideas, values, behaviors, and inter-actions that coalesce into policies and institutions. Sustained by common-ality and continuation, they evolve in response to population growth; environmental factors; changing relations with neighboring societies (Diamond, 1997, 2005); and as ideas, values, and plans build and shift. Just as the flut-tering wings of a butterfly in a Brazilian rain forest affect the ecology of the planet, everyone is partly responsible for the nature of society. Because pro-grams aim to improve society (or some corner of it) and evaluations aim to improve programs, evaluators bear a unique social responsibility.

Traditionally, evaluators have mostly been aware of their responsibili-ties to clients and of legal responsibilities specified in contracts. From a postmodern perspective, this makes evaluators the hired lackeys of those who can afford to pay them. What of stakeholders who are harmed or intended beneficiaries who fail to benefit from a program? From a tradi-tional perspective, acting on the interests of stakeholders other than clients may amount to advocacy, roughly the evaluator's equivalent of an ethnog-rapher's "going native." Depending on circumstances, advocacy is some-times justifiable but, other times, tantamount to professional irresponsibility (Scriven, 1997; Scriven, Greene, Stake, & Mabry, 1995). Advocacy might also promote not the rights and interests of stakeholder groups, but social values. Advocacy for social values is more abstract and, to the degree that values can be challenged (e.g., by the left or the right), potentially more contentious: *whose view of societal values should be pursued?* Urging social values would predicate defining them, which itself would invite charges of undue author-ity and surely involve the conscious or unconscious promotion of personal values.

Few evaluators see themselves as values-setters or social engineers, yet increasingly evaluators are seeking opportunities to influence public policy (Henry & Mark, 2003; Kirkhart, 2000; Weiss, 1999; Weiss, Murphy-Graham, & Birkeland, 2005). Some evaluators expect their work to influence social policy and governmental structures, and some have devised respected means for doing so (Chelimsky, 2007; Datta, 2007). Yet even they might object to evaluation practice with the *a priori* goal of social reform (Chelimsky & Shadish, 1997; Scriven, 1997).

Evaluators who would disparage critical social theory evaluators might do well to consider whether the latter are merely more obviously, more con-sciously, more deliberately engaged in societal restructuring than they themselves. Any evaluator may "argue for the data" (Smith, personal com-munication, 1997) in encouraging appropriate use, but critical social the-ory evaluators are more likely to be aware that their arguments have ideological edges, infused with their own sense of social responsibility. And they are more a social cause as looming larger than responsibility to clients, to right-to-know and need-to-know audiences, or to the professional guild (Smith, 1998). This enlarged sense of responsibility comes at a cost.

Professional Compensation

"For every grain of wit there is a grain of folly. For every thing you have missed, you have gained something else; and for every thing you gain, you lose something," or so Emerson (1841/1903) advised in his essay on Compensation. With the "wit" that critical social theory evaluation may give evaluators to deepen understanding of societal responsibility comes the potential for "folly."

The development of critical social theory evaluation may be seen as a gain for the profession, adding to an expanding methodological repertoire and, in so doing, encouraging further innovation. Articulating a new approach makes it available for use as needed (see American Evaluation Association, 2003; Chelimsky, 2007). This particular approach complements existing efforts by evaluators to engage in the policy arena, giving the profession not only a data-based point of entry, but also an ideological one. Denial of critical social theory evaluation would constitute an opportunity cost to the profession.

But critical social theory evaluation also presents a potential for professional loss. The threat is discernible in evaluators' arguments against advocacy, traditional concerns about bias, postmodern concerns about undue assumptions of authority, and politico-professional concerns about revolution, each of which menaces the credibility of the profession. Thus, the profession's acceptance of critical social theory evaluation could pose a different kind of opportunity cost, also affecting evaluation's viability as a player on the policy stage.

Societal Compensation

Costs and compensations to society should also be considered. Clients and societies expect evaluation findings to be valid in the sense represented in the Accuracy Standards, not in the sense of catalytic validity, the capacity to foment change (Lather, 1993). If an evaluation's results are easily dismissed as perspective or political manifesto, then evaluation's indirect opportunity to improve society is lost in the seeking of a more direct opportunity through critical social theory evaluation. Obversely, denial of critical social theory evaluation would impose on society the loss of champions of its values and of human and social interests often threatened by economic interests and the self-aggrandizement of the powerful.

Individual Compensation

The costs of critical social theory evaluation fall not only on the profession as a whole but also, of course, on critical social theory evaluators individually.

NEW DIRECTIONS FOR EVALUATION • DOI: 10.1002/ev

Each must gird for opposition from clients and colleagues and decide whether the satisfactions of fighting the good fight compensate for its searing wounds. Or, one may renounce critical social theory evaluation and decide whether a sense of social irresponsibility is even more searing. Or, as some of the examples of critical social theory evaluation in this volume illustrate, perhaps an evaluator may also strategically respond to circumstances that call for critical perspectives in the service of society.

Conclusion

Where's the dragon? That depends on the viewing trajectory. The potential costs of critical social theory evaluation to society, to the profession, and to individual evaluators are substantial, and it is no wonder that they incite resistance. For those worried that critical social theory evaluation could cost the profession its credibility, could cost society access to credible evaluation data, and could cost individual evaluators their prestige and livelihoods, critical social theory evaluation is the dragon, a fire-breathing imminent threat. For them, an appropriate response would be to slay critical social theory evaluation as too ideologically driven, too politically driven to be considered evaluation at all.

For evaluators concerned about the social threats they encounter as they evaluate programs, the dragon is to be found in the persons, policies, and institutions that jeopardize human and social values. For these challengers, the opportunity that critical social theory evaluation presents is grand: a more direct path to exercise one's obligations as a citizen while simultaneously exercising one's obligations as an evaluator. From this point of view, critical social theory evaluation is one way that evaluators can help to slay the dragons that threaten societal values.

References

Adorno, T. W. (1978). *Minima moralia: Reflections on a damaged life* (E.F.N. Jephcott, Trans.). New York: Verso.

American Evaluation Association. (1995). Guiding principles for evaluators. In W. R. Shadish, D. L. Newman, M. A. Scheirer, & C. Wye (Eds.), *Guiding principles for evaluators. New Directions for Program Evaluation, 66,* 19–26.

American Evaluation Association. (2003, November). *Response to U.S. Department of Education notice of proposed priority, "Scientifically Based Evaluation Methods"* (Federal Register RIN 1890-ZA00, November 4, 2003). Retrieved December 4, 2009, from http://www.eval.org/doestatement.htm

American Psychological Association. (2007). *Ethical principles of psychologists and code of conduct.* Washington, DC: Author. Retrieved July 5, 2006, from http://www.apa .org/ethics/code2002.html

American Sociological Association. (1997). *Code of ethics.* Washington, DC: Author. Retrieved July 5, 2006, from http://www2.asanet.org/members/ecoderev.html

Banks, J. A. (2006). *Race, culture, and education: The selected works of James A. Banks.* London: Routledge.

Baudrillard, J. (1983). *Simulations* (P. Foss, P. Patton, & J. Johnston, Trans.). New York: Semiotest(e).

Bleier, R. (Ed.). (1986). *Feminists approach to science*. Elmsford, New York: Pergamon.

Bloom, B. S., Englehart, M. D., Furst, G. J., Hill, W. H., & Krathwohl, D. R. (1956). *Taxonomy of educational objectives: Handbook I, the cognitive domain*. New York: David McKay.

Chelimsky, E. (2007). Factors influencing the choice of methods in federal evaluation practice. In G. Julnes & D. Rog (Eds.), *Informing federal policies on evaluation methodology: Building the evidence base for method choice in government sponsored evaluation. New Directions for Evaluation, 113*, 13–33.

Chelimsky, E., & Shadish, W. R. (Eds.). (1997). *Evaluation for the 21st century: A handbook*. Thousand Oaks, CA: Sage.

Christie, C. A., & Alkin, M. C. (2005). Objectives-based evaluation. In S. Mathison (Ed.), *Encyclopedia of evaluation* (p. 284). Newbury Park, CA: Sage.

Compte, I.A.M.F.X. (1851–54, ed. 1898/2002). *Système de politique positive* [System of positive polity]. Paris: Thoemmes Continuum.

Cronbach, L. J. (1975). Beyond the two disciplines of scientific psychology. *American Psychologist, 30*, 116–127.

Datta, L. (2007). Looking at the evidence: What variations in practice might indicate. In G. Julnes & D. Rog (Eds.), *Informing federal policies on evaluation methodology: Building the evidence base for method choice in government sponsored evaluation. New Directions for Evaluation, 113*, 35–54.

Derrida, J. (1976). *On grammatology* (G. Spivak, Trans.). Baltimore: Johns Hopkins University Press.

Diamond, J. (1997). *Guns, germs, and steel: The fates of human societies*. New York: W. W. Norton.

Diamond, J. (2005). *Collapse: How societies choose to fail or succeed*. New York: Penguin.

Emerson, R. W. (1841/1903). *Essays: First series*. Boston: Houghton, Mifflin & Co.

Fetterman, D. M. (1996). *Empowerment evaluation: Knowledge and tools for self-assessment and accountability*. Thousand Oaks, CA: Sage.

Foucault, M. (1973). *The order of things: An archaeology of the human sciences*. New York: Vintage Books.

Foucault, M. (1980). *Power/knowledge*. Cambridge, MA: Harvard University Press.

Frijda, N. H. (1986). *The emotions*. New York: Cambridge University Press.

Greene, J. C. (1997). Participatory evaluation. In L. Mabry (Ed.), *Evaluation and the postmodern dilemma* (pp. 171–189). Greenwich, CT: JAI Press.

Greene, J. C. (2006). Evaluation, democracy, and social change. In I. F. Shaw, J. Greene, & M. Mark (Eds.), *The Sage handbook of evaluation* (pp. 118–140). Thousand Oaks, CA: Sage.

Greene, M. (1994). Postmodernism and the crisis of representation. *English Education, 26*(4), 206–219.

Guba, E. G. (1978). *Toward a methodology of naturalistic inquiry in educational evaluation* (Monograph 8). Los Angeles: UCLA Center for the Study of Evaluation.

Guba, E. G. (1990). *The paradigm dialog*. Thousand Oaks, CA: Sage.

Guba, E. G., & Lincoln, Y. S. (1989). *Fourth generation evaluation*. Thousand Oaks, CA: Sage.

Habermas, J. (1975). *Legitimation crisis* (T. McCarthy, Trans.). Boston: Beacon Press.

Habermas, J. (1987). *The philosophical discourse of modernity* (F. Lawrence, Trans.). Cambridge, MA: MIT Press.

Henry, G. T., & Mark, M. M. (2003). Beyond use: Understanding evaluation's influence on attitudes and actions. *American Journal of Evaluation, 24*(3), 293–314.

House, E. R. (1993). *Professional evaluation: Social impact and political consequences*. Newbury Park, CA: Sage.

House, E. R. (1995). Principled evaluation: A critique of the AEA Guiding Principles. In W. R. Shadish, D. L. Newman, M. A. Scheirer, & C. Wye (Eds.), *Guiding principles for evaluators. New Directions for Program Evaluation, 66*, 27–34.

House, E. R., & Howe, K. R. (1999). *Values in evaluation and social research.* Thousand Oaks, CA: Sage.

Joint Committee on Standards for Educational Evaluation. (1994). *The program evaluation standards: How to assess evaluations of educational programs* (2nd ed.). Thousand Oaks, CA: Sage.

Kimmel, A. J. (1988). *Ethics and values in applied social research.* Thousand Oaks, CA: Sage.

King, J., Stevahn, L., Ghere, G., & Minnema, J. (2001). Toward a taxonomy of essential evaluator competencies. *American Journal of Evaluation, 22*(2), 229–247.

Kirkhart, K. E. (1981). Defining evaluator competencies: New light on an old issue. *American Journal of Evaluation, 2*(2), 188–192.

Kirkhart, K. E. (2000). Reconceptualizing evaluation use: An integrated theory of influence. In V. J. Caracelli &. H. Preskill (Eds.), *The expanding scope of evaluation use. New Directions for Evaluation, 88*, 5–23.

Lather, P. (1991). *Feminist research in education: Within/against.* Geelong, Australia: Deakin University Press.

Lather, P. (1993). Fertile obsession: Validity after poststructuralism. *Sociological Quarterly, 34*(4), 673–693.

Lyotard, J. F. (1979/1984). *The postmodern condition: A report on knowledge* (G. Bennington & B. Massumi, Trans.). Minneapolis: University of Minnesota Press.

Mabry, L. (1997). Implicit and explicit advocacy in postmodern evaluation. In L. Mabry (Ed.), *Evaluation and the postmodern dilemma* (pp. 191–203). Greenwich, CT: JAI Press.

Mabry, L. (1999). Circumstantial ethics. *American Journal of Evaluation, 20*(2), 199–212.

Mabry, L. (2008). Ethics for social science in postmodern times. In D. Mertens & P. Ginsberg (Eds.), *Handbook of social research ethics.* Newbury Park, CA: Sage.

Mabry, L. (in press). The responsibility of evaluation. In W. Boettcher (Ed.), *Education, evaluation, and society.* Berlin: Waxmann.

Mabry, L., & Ettinger, L. (1999). Supporting community-oriented educational change: Case and analysis. *Education Policy Analysis Archives, 7*(14).

Marx, K., & Engels, F. (1867/1996). *Das kapital.* Chicago: H. Regnery.

Mauthner, M., Birch, M., Jessop, J., & Miller, T. (2002). *Ethics in qualitative research.* London: Sage.

Mertens, D. M. (2005). *Research and evaluation in education and psychology: Integrating diversity with quantitative, qualitative, and mixed methods* (2nd ed.). Thousand Oaks, CA: Sage.

Mill, J. S. (1863/1891). *Utilitarianism.* London: Longmans, Green, & Co.

Newman, D. L., & Brown, R. D. (1996). *Applied ethics for program evaluation.* Thousand Oaks, CA: Sage.

Ogbu, J. U. (1978). *Minority education and caste: The American system in cross-cultural perspective.* San Diego: Academic Press.

Ortony, A., Clore, G. L., & Collins, A. (1988). *The cognitive structure of emotions.* Cambridge, UK: Cambridge University Press.

Patton, M. Q. (1997). *Utilization-focused evaluation* (3rd ed.). Thousand Oaks, CA: Sage.

Rawls, J. (1971). *A theory of justice.* Cambridge, MA: Harvard University Press.

Rosenau, P. R. (1992). *Postmodernism and the social sciences: Insights, inroads, and intrusions.* Princeton, NJ: Princeton University Press.

Rousseau, J. J. (1755/1992). *Discourse on inequality.* Paris: G. F. Flammarion.

Sartre, J. P. (1944). *Huis clos* [No exit] (S. Gilbert, Trans.). New York: Vintage.

Scriven, M. (1972). Pros and cons about goal-free evaluation. *Evaluation Comment, 3*(4), 1–3.

Scriven, M. (1997). Truth and objectivity in evaluation. In E. Chelimsky & W. R. Shadish (Eds.), *Evaluation for the 21st century: A handbook* (pp. 477–500). Thousand Oaks, CA: Sage.

Scriven, M. (1998, November). *An evaluation dilemma: Change agent vs. analyst.* Paper presented at the annual meeting of the American Evaluation Association, Chicago.

Scriven, M., Greene, J., Stake, R., & Mabry, L. (1995, November). *Advocacy for our clients: The necessary evil in evaluation?* Panel presentation to the International Evaluation Conference, Vancouver, BC.

Shadish, W. R., Jr., Cook, T. D., & Leviton, L. C. (1991). *Foundations of program evaluation: Theories of practice.* Newbury Park, CA: Sage.

Smith, N. (1998). Professional reasons for declining an evaluation contract. *American Journal of Evaluation, 19*(2), 177–190.

Stufflebeam, D. L. (1987). The CIPP model for program evaluation. In G. F. Madaus, M. S. Scriven, & D. L. Stufflebeam (Eds.), *Evaluation models: Viewpoints on educational and human services evaluation* (pp. 117–141). Boston: Kluwer-Nijhoff.

Stufflebeam, D. L. (1994). Empowerment evaluation, objectivist evaluation, and evaluation standards: Where the future of evaluation should not go and where it needs to go. *Evaluation Practice, 15*(3), 321–338.

Stufflebeam, D. L. (Ed.) (2001). *Evaluation models. New Directions for Evaluation, 89.*

Stufflebeam, D. L., Madaus, G. F., & Kellaghan, T. (Eds.). (2000). *Evaluation models: Viewpoints on educational and human services evaluation* (2nd ed.). Dordrecht, Netherlands: Kluwer.

Stufflebeam, D. S., Patton, M. Q., Fetterman, D., Greene, J. G., Scriven, M. S., & Mabry, L. (2001, November). *Theories of action in program evaluation.* Panel presentation at the annual meeting of the American Evaluation Association, St. Louis.

Sutton, M. (1998). Feminist epistemology and research methods. In N. P. Stromquist (Ed.), *Women in the third world: An encyclopedia of contemporary issues* (pp. 13–23). New York: Garland.

Walker, D. (1997). Why won't they listen? Reflections of a formative evaluator. In L. Mabry (Ed.), *Evaluation and the postmodern dilemma* (pp. 121–137). Greenwich, CT: JAI Press.

Weiss, C. H. (1999). The interface between evaluation and public policy action. *Evaluation, 5*(4), 468–486.

Weiss, C. H., Murphy-Graham, E., & Birkeland, S. (2005). An alternate route to policy influence. *American Journal of Evaluation, 26*(1), 12–30.

LINDA MABRY *is a professor of educational psychology at Washington State University Vancouver and president-elect of the Oregon Program Evaluators Network.*

INDEX

NEW DIRECTIONS FOR EVALUATION
ORDER FORM SUBSCRIPTION AND SINGLE ISSUES

DISCOUNTED BACK ISSUES:

Use this form to receive 20% off all back issues of *New Directions for Evaluation*.
All single issues priced at **$23.20** (normally $29.00)

TITLE   ISSUE NO.   ISBN

_____   _____   _____

_____   _____   _____

_____   _____   _____

Call 888-378-2537 or see mailing instructions below. When calling, mention the promotional code JBNND to receive your discount. For a complete list of issues, please visit www.josseybass.com/go/ev

SUBSCRIPTIONS: (1 YEAR, 4 ISSUES)

☐ New Order   ☐ Renewal

U.S.	☐ Individual: $89	☐ Institutional: $271
CANADA/MEXICO	☐ Individual: $89	☐ Institutional: $311
ALL OTHERS	☐ Individual: $113	☐ Institutional: $345

Call 888-378-2537 or see mailing and pricing instructions below.
Online subscriptions are available at www.onlinelibrary.wiley.com

ORDER TOTALS:

Issue / Subscription Amount: $ _____

Shipping Amount: $ _____
(for single issues only – subscription prices include shipping)

Total Amount: $ _____

SHIPPING CHARGES:	
First Item	$5.00
Each Add'l Item	$3.00

(No sales tax for U.S. subscriptions. Canadian residents, add GST for subscription orders. Individual rate subscriptions must be paid by personal check or credit card. Individual rate subscriptions may not be resold as library copies.)

BILLING & SHIPPING INFORMATION:

☐ **PAYMENT ENCLOSED:** *(U.S. check or money order only. All payments must be in U.S. dollars.)*

☐ **CREDIT CARD:**   ☐ VISA   ☐ MC   ☐ AMEX

Card number _____ Exp. Date _____

Card Holder Name _____ Card Issue # _____

Signature _____ Day Phone _____

☐ **BILL ME:** *(U.S. institutional orders only. Purchase order required.)*

Purchase order # _____
Federal Tax ID 13559302 • GST 89102-8052

Name _____

Address _____

Phone _____ E-mail _____

Copy or detach page and send to: **John Wiley & Sons, PTSC, 5th Floor**
                                   989 Market Street, San Francisco, CA 94103-1741

Order Form can also be faxed to: **888-481-2665**

PROMO JBNND